CREATIVE BIBLE LESSONS
IN NEHEMIAH

12 SESSIONS ON DISCOVERING WHAT LEADERSHIP MEANS FOR STUDENTS TODAY

PERFECT FOR SUNDAY SCHOOL, YOUTH MEETINGS, SMALL GROUPS, AND MORE!

ANDREW HEDGES

ZONDERVAN™

GRAND RAPIDS, MICHIGAN 49530 USA

Youth Specialties

www.youthspecialties.com

CREATIVE BIBLE LESSONS IN NEHEMIAH

12 SESSIONS ON DISCOVERING WHAT LEADERSHIP MEANS FOR STUDENTS TODAY

ANDREW HEDGES

Creative Bible Lessons in Nehemiah:12 sessions on discovering what leadership means for students today
Copyright © 2005 by Youth Specialties

Youth Specialties Products, 300 South Pierce Street, El Cajon, CA 92020, are published by Zondervan,
5300 Patterson Avenue SE, Grand Rapids, MI 49530

Library of Congress Cataloging-in-Publication Data
Hedges, Andrew A., 1977-
  Creative Bible lessons in Nehemiah : 12 sessions on discovering what leadership means for students today / by
Andrew A. Hedges.
      p. cm. -- (Creative Bible lessons)
  ISBN 0-310-25880-4 (pbk.)
  1. Bible. O.T. Nehemiah--Study and teaching (Secondary) 2. Christian education of teenagers. I. Title. II. Series.
  BS1365.55.H43 2005
  222'.8'00712--dc22
                                                                                                        2004030063

Editorial direction by Dave Urbanski
Edited by Laura Gross
Proofread by Janie Wilkerson and Kristi Robison
Cover design by Holly Sharp
Interior design by Mark Novelli
Printed in the United States of America

08 09 10 / VGM / 10 9 8 7 6 5 4 3

DEDICATION

To Cara and Anna—
Your love and support continues to spur me on to be a better husband and father to the glory of God. This book would not have happened without you!

To Dr. Thomas Hutchison—
Your example of biblical leadership and your ability to meet students where they are have been my model for teaching leadership to young people.

TABLE OF CONTENTS

INTRODUCTION

INTRODUCTION

TRAINING YOUNG LEADERS

As we study leaders in various venues, we find that many are in their teens and twenties—yet we normally label this age group the "leaders of tomorrow." Remarkably, they have shown themselves to be the leaders of today. However, the vast majority of them lack Christian values. These actors, musicians, and others with power and influence are making their marks in the world with their beliefs.

Many young believers look at these celebrities in awe and desire to be leaders in some capacity as well. We as youth workers must invest in their lives, equip them with skills, and provide opportunities for them to strengthen and stretch their leadership muscles and to be the leaders we so desperately need in our communities, schools, and churches—indeed, all around the world.

My passion is training young people to lead for the cause of Christ, and this curriculum does just that. But leadership takes many forms. It's just as important that young believers—whether or not they ever lead in an official or prominent capacity—develop leadership skills they'll most definitely need later in life to further the kingdom of God. And this curriculum does just that as well.

I've found a wonderful example of leadership in the life of Nehemiah. The lessons from this man's life can very practically equip young leaders with the knowledge and skills needed to be strong, biblical leaders in whatever capacities they encounter.

This study provides a focused approach to understanding some of the basic building blocks of true biblical leadership, as well as a setting for students to brainstorm and dream about how they can be leaders right now and right where they are.

Charles Swindoll, in his book *Hand Me Another Brick*, writes, "There is one book, written about 425 B.C., that looms as a classic work on effective leadership; yet it is strangely obscure and virtually unknown to people of today. It was written by a man who was prominent in business and politics in the ancient Middle East. He not only possessed an exceptional personal philosophy of leadership, but he *lived it out* as well. In his lifetime, this gentleman rose from total obscurity to national recognition. His book bears his name: Nehemiah."[1]

This is the message students need to hear, and I believe they can emulate Nehemiah's example and begin to develop their leadership potential.

My desire is to provide you with a creative approach to teaching leadership principles and at the same time give your students practical ways of implementing each principle. This particular curriculum offers a lot of Bible study as well as activities and hints on how to reach all of the students in a particular group. With *Creative Bible Lessons in Nehemiah*, you can begin to see and relate to your students on their level as well as teach Scripture in ways that meet their learning styles.

This study not only will contribute to students' personal development, but it also will benefit the future of our churches as we equip and train our "leaders of tomorrow"…today.

Following Christ,

Andrew A. Hedges

[1] Swindoll, Charles R. *Hand Me Another Brick*. (Nashville: Word Publishing, 1998), 2.

LEARNING HOW YOUR STUDENTS LEARN

In order to understand how to most effectively use this book, it's important to know the philosophy behind it. In the same way, in order to teach your students effectively, you need to know how they learn. In her book, *Learning Styles: Reaching Everyone God Gave You to Teach*, Marlene LeFever does a marvelous job of providing insight into how people learn. As a teacher or parent, it would be well worth your time to check out this book. For the time being, the following paragraphs will provide a basic understanding of certain terms.

IMAGINATIVE LEARNERS

These are "feeling" people who get involved with others and learn best in settings that encourage the development of interpersonal relationships. These curious, questioning learners gain knowledge by listening and sharing ideas. They see the big picture much more easily than the small details. They learn by sensing, feeling, watching. They can see all sides of the issues presented.[2]

ANALYTIC LEARNERS

They also learn by watching and listening. They view a teacher as the primary information giver, and they sit and carefully assess the value of the information presented. These students learn in the way most teachers have traditionally taught, and so they are often considered the best learners. They are strategic planners, and they aim for perfection—the right answers, *the A's* in school and in life. These learners want all the data before they make a decision.[3]

COMMON SENSE LEARNERS

They like to play with ideas to see if they are rational and workable. These students want to test theory in the real world, to apply what has been learned. They love to get the job done. They are hands-on people who, using their own ideas, can analyze problems and solve or fix them. Common Sense Learners, as the name suggests, excel when dealing with what is practical and of immediate importance to them. They learn best when learning is combined with doing.[4]

DYNAMIC LEARNERS

They also enjoy action as part of the learning process, but rather than thinking projects through to their rational conclusions, Dynamic Learners excel in following hunches and sensing new directions and possibilities. These risk takers thrive

[2] LeFever, Marlene. D. *Learning Styles: Reaching Everyone God Gave You to Teach.* (Colorado Springs, CO: David C. Cook Publishing Co., 1995), 20.
[3] Ibid, 20. [4] Ibid, 20.

on situations that call for flexibility and change and find real joy in starting something new or putting their personal stamp of originality on an idea.[5]

God made each of us in wonderfully unique ways, including the way we learn. These four basic learning styles provide only a glimpse of how students learn during any given session in this book—because within each learning style, you will also find students who learn best through auditory, visual, or tactile/kinesthetic means.[6] You may have an Imaginative Learner who seems to respond more to pictures or videos. A Common Sense Learner may fit into a more tactile/kinesthetic or hands-on style, while another prefers to sit and listen to a tape or a guest lecturer. Each student has a different combination by which he or she learns best.

As you use this curriculum, the best place to start is with yourself. Take time to read over the learning styles again to see where you fit and consider whether you are more auditory, visual, or tactile/kinesthetic. Which one seems to describe you best? Just keep in mind that most teachers teach the way they learn best. Therefore you will need to concentrate on reaching all of the learning styles found within your group of students. For your benefit, however, this curriculum has been designed so you can reach all four learning styles in each session.

HOW TO USE THIS BOOK

You'll find each session is designed not only to reach students who fall under all four learning styles, but also to allow options for you to choose the right combinations for your students by way of learning preferences—auditory, visual, and tactile/kinesthetic. Each of these learning activities is labeled to help you see which style and preference is strongest for each activity. However, some of the learning activities may cross over or combine several styles and preferences. The idea is to work out the best scenario for your particular group. The following paragraphs will provide brief explanations of the session segments.

OVERVIEW

This is a simple statement describing the learning objective for the session.

OPENER

The first activity of each session is designed as an attention grabber. Of course, your Imaginative Learners will be at the fore of each of these events. Imaginative Learners get excited about talking things out and providing direction for what's to come, so the Opener is likely their time to shine. Again, options are provided to

[5] Ibid, 21. [6] Ibid, 32.

meet the strongest learning preferences you find in your students. The Appendix includes verses of Scripture your students might want to memorize, as they will tie together the focus of each particular session. In fact, you may want to incorporate a weekly Scripture memory program to go along with your study.

YOU'LL NEED

A handy list of all the possible materials you may need for each portion of the session is provided for your benefit.

IN THE WORD

During this activity the Analytic Learners do their thing. (This may be the easiest section for you as well, since this is the most typical teaching method.) Background information and a creative outline of the passage for study are provided here so you can tailor a presentation of the passage to fit your group. You'll also find a particular focus for the theme of each passage. Pay special attention to the parenthetical notes scattered throughout the Bible study outlines—they are great primers for deeper questions you may want to ask in addition to the questions found in *Taking Another Look* and *A Final Word*.

TAKING ANOTHER LOOK

Common Sense Learners excel at applying small group discussion or other activities to real life. This section may be tied to the next segment in order to put into practice the information discussed. You'll want to consider this as you decide between your activity options.

PRACTICAL EXPERIENCE

Finally, the Dynamic Learners can take off running. This segment provides an opportunity to show where the theme of the session can go after the study time is over. The activities here may prove to be of great practical benefit for your youth group, family times, or community events. This segment is the time when everything comes together, and students begin moving from their dreams of leadership to actually making things happen.

A FINAL WORD

The last section contains summary questions designed to assess whether or not all the learning styles have been reached and how the session went overall. You may be able to use these times to consider any changes you may wish to make to your next session or evaluate the areas in which your students are strongest.

One final note about the sections concerns the duration of each learning activity. If you were to choose to do the minimum for each section, the sessions are designed to fit within a one-hour time frame. However, the amount of time it takes will differ according to the size and makeup of your group. As you have time, you should feel free to use as many of the learning activities as you can. The more material you cover, the more opportunities your students will have to gain knowledge within their respective learning styles and preferences. The choice is yours.

This book is designed to help all students and youth workers—regardless of previous knowledge or learning styles—become the leaders they can be for the cause of Christ. May God be with you all as you start laying the building blocks for biblical leadership.

OVERVIEW

This session is designed to show the necessity of prayer in the life of a godly leader. During this session students will

- Be able to recognize the priority of prayer
- Understand how to pray effectively
- Practice praying for each other

OPENER (5 MINUTES)

OPTION 1: HOW NOT TO DO IT [IMAGINATIVE, VISUAL]

Start 00:24:00 Exterior view of a house at night; fades to a scene where the family is sitting around the dinner table.

Stop 00:26:16 Jack (Robert De Niro) says, "Thank you, Greg. That was interesting, too."

YOU'LL NEED

- *Meet the Parents* DVD (Universal Pictures, 2000)
- TV and DVD player

In this scene, Greg Focker (Ben Stiller) is put on the spot when his girlfriend's father, whom he's meeting for the first time, asks Greg to pray before their meal. After the clip finishes, start a discussion with the following questions—

* **How do you think Greg did with his prayer?**
* **What was he praying about?**
* **Does his prayer remind you of prayers you've heard or maybe even prayed yourself?**

Transition into the next part by saying something like

While this depiction of prayer is funny, the sad truth is that many Christians would not pray with any more passion or purpose. If you are going to be an effective leader, then you need to know how to pray effectively. James 5:16 says, "The prayer of a righteous man is powerful and effective." Nehemiah was a leader who knew how to pray effectively.

OPTION 2: JUST ANOTHER PRAYER [IMAGINATIVE, AUDITORY]

Have students share some of the prayers they learned in childhood or ones they've heard friends or relatives say—especially around mealtimes. Most students will remember prayers like, "God is great" and "Now I lay me down to sleep," but they may be able to share some other common prayers as well.

After your students have shared a few examples, say something like

These prayers are good, but why do we pray them? Do we pray the way the Bible teaches us to pray? While we think of general prayer as a good thing, many Christians pray without even knowing why they pray—or without any passion or purpose. Effective leaders know how to pray effectively. James 5:16 says, "The prayer of a righteous man is powerful and effective." Nehemiah was a leader who knew how to pray effectively.

IN THE WORD (15 MINUTES)

[ANALYTICAL, AUDITORY]

SETTING

YOU'LL NEED

• Bibles

* The book of Nehemiah begins in the fifth century B.C.
* The month refers to November and December on our calendars.
* Susa was the capital and royal city of the Persian Empire (modern-day Iran).
* The book of Esther also takes place here.

- The city was strongly fortified, so Nehemiah would have known how to build a strong wall.

BACKGROUND

- King Artaxerxes I was in power, and he may have been the king during Esther's time.
- Ezra also lived during the time of Nehemiah. Ezra's focus was on the temple, and Nehemiah was more focused on the wall because the city had been without protection for 90 years.
- Nehemiah was the cupbearer to the king (verse 11). The cupbearer's job was a risky one. He tasted the king's wine and the food before the king ate his meals. If the food or drink was poisoned—no more cupbearer, and long live the king! The cupbearer was, according to history, one of the most influential people in the king's court.

BASIC OUTLINE

I. Nehemiah Provides the Setting for the Encounter (vv. 1-2)

II. Nehemiah Receives the Message (v. 3)

    A. The Jews are in great trouble.

    B. The wall of Jerusalem is broken down.

    C. The gates of Jerusalem are burned down.

    (Note: Babylon, led by King Nebuchadnezzar, leveled Jerusalem in 586 B.C. and took the Jews captive.)

III. Nehemiah Responds to the Message (vv. 4-11)

(Note: Pay close attention to the order of his prayer, as well as what was included in it.)

    A. He prepares his mind and heart; he sits, weeps, mourns, and fasts.

    B. He prays.

        1. He recognizes who God is.

        (Note: When God chose Nehemiah to help and protect his people, he picked a man who had a proper understanding of and respect for God. God's protection and provision for his people are the themes of the entire book of Nehemiah.)

        2. He confesses sin.

            a. Nehemiah confesses the sins of the people.

            b. Nehemiah confesses his own sins.

3. He claims the promise of God.

4. Nehemiah asks God to protect him.

(Note: Nehemiah considers himself a servant—or "right before God.")

TAKING ANOTHER LOOK (15 MINUTES)

OPTION 1: PRAYER-LIB [COMMON SENSE, VISUAL]

YOU'LL NEED
• Copies of **Prayer Lib** repro page (page 20-21), one for each small group
• Pens or pencils

This is a fun ad-lib activity that will give some perspective on how Nehemiah prayed. Hand each student a copy of the **Prayer-Lib** repro page (page 20-21) and something to write with. Give your students time to fill in the blanks, and then ask some of your students to share their prayers with the rest of the group.

OPTION 2: THINKING LIKE A LEADER [COMMON SENSE, AUDITORY]

YOU'LL NEED
• Copies of **Thinking Like a Leader** repro page (page 22), one for each small group
• Pens or pencils

Have students break into smaller groups. Hand each group a copy of the **Thinking Like a Leader** repro page (page 22) and something to write with. Allow the groups some time to answer the questions. When most have finished, ask each group to share a couple of its answers with everyone.

PRACTICAL EXPERIENCE (15 MINUTES)

[DYNAMIC, KINESTHETIC]

YOU'LL NEED
• A ball of yarn for each small group

This activity shows in a concrete way how prayer connects us to each other and how God can use our prayers to touch those around us. Have your students remain in their small groups and sit in circles. Give one person in each group a ball of yarn. The first person should share a prayer request with the group and then, while still holding one end of the yarn, toss the rest of the ball to someone sitting across from him. The person who catches the yarn prays for the last person's request and, in turn, shares a request of her own before tossing it back across the circle. As the yarn ball makes its way around the circle, a web formation will appear. Eventually, the yarn should be tossed back to the first person, and he closes in prayer.

A FINAL WORD (10 MINUTES)

Have a short discussion with your students and ask the following questions—

* **Why is it important to pray effectively?**
* **What does Nehemiah's prayer—the order of his prayer and what he included—teach us about prayer?**
* **Can praying like we just did with the yarn make a difference? Why?**
* **Nehemiah's prayer shows he considers himself a servant. How do you think servanthood relates to leadership?**
* **What is something we can do as a group to keep praying for each other the way we should?**

CLOSING PRAYER

Wrap up your time with a prayer like

God,

It's great that we've had the chance to talk through lots of ideas for making our prayers more effective, but committing to actually doing these things is completely different. Please help us pray effectively and fervently from this day on.

Amen.

PRAYER-LIB

PART 1

Write your answers to the following statements in the blanks provided. When you are finished, copy your answers on the blank lines with the corresponding numbers in part 2 on the next page.

1. A name you call God in prayer:_____

2. An adjective for God:_____

3. An adjective for God:_____

4. A time of day:_____

5. The name of your group:_____

6. The name of your town:_____

7. A favorite promise found in Scripture:_____

8. Your leader's name:_____

PRAYER-LIB

PART 2

Adaptation of Nehemiah 1:5-11

"O _____, God of heaven,
           1

the _____ and
           2

_____God, who keeps his covenant
           3

of love with those who love him and obey his commands, let your ear be attentive

and your eyes open to hear the prayer your servant is praying before you _____

_____ for
           4

_____, the people of
           5

_____. I confess the sins we
           6

[Christians], including myself and my father's house, have committed against you.

We have acted very wickedly toward you. We have not obeyed the commands,

decrees and laws you gave [in your Word]. Remember the instruction you gave [in

your Word], saying, '_____
                      7

_____'.

_____ are your servants and your
           5

people, whom you redeemed by your great strength and your mighty hand.

O _____, let your ear be attentive
   1

to the prayer of this your servant and to the prayer of your servants who delight in

revering your name. Give your servant success today by granting him [or her] favor

in the presence of _____."
                   8

THINKING LIKE A LEADER

1. What caused Nehemiah to pray?

2. For whom did Nehemiah pray?

3. How did Nehemiah's gifts and experiences relate to his prayer?

4. How did Nehemiah prepare for his prayer?

5. Why is Nehemiah's process of praying important?

6. How does Nehemiah's prayer compare to the prayers you hear these days?

7. Do you regularly take time to prepare before you pray? Why might that be important to do in order to get ready?

8. What does God think about praying for your own needs?

9. What could you pray for now, in light of your gifts and abilities?

10. Looking at Nehemiah's example, how often should you pray?

A LEADER PREPARES A PLAN
SESSION 2: NEHEMIAH 2

OVERVIEW

The focus of this session is preparation.

During this session students will

- Learn to identify their needs and the needs of those they may lead
- Understand how to obtain the necessities for meeting these needs and implementing their plans
- Begin preparing themselves for fulfilling God's purposes for their lives and those they lead

OPENER (10 MINUTES)

OPTION 1: ONLY THE NECESSITIES [IMAGINATIVE, VISUAL]

Place on a table some items that you might take on a backpacking trip. You could also throw in a few random items as well. Tell your students they can choose only five items to take with them on a long hike through the mountains. Have them work in pairs to come up with a list of items they would take on their journeys. Let them

YOU'LL NEED

- Items you would take along on a backpacking trip (e.g., compass, rope, flashlight, canteen)

- Sheets of paper, one for each pair of students

- Pencils or pens

know they should be prepared to support their choices, though there are no right or wrong answers. When they finish, discuss the items they chose to take with them.

Questions to ask—

- **How did you go about making your final choices?**
- **How difficult was it to decide what to take with you?**
- **Why is it important to take time to think through what you'd need and prepare before a trip like this?**

Now say something like

Just like preparing for a trip, we need to be sure we are prepared for each and every day, especially if we lead others. Nehemiah thought through what he needed to accomplish in his tasks, and he knew how to go about getting what he needed. 1 Corinthians 14:40 says, "But everything should be done in a fitting and orderly way." Nehemiah was a leader who knew that preparation is the key to motivating people to follow.

OPTION 2: EGG DROP [IMAGINATIVE, KINESTHETIC]

YOU'LL NEED

• Eggs, one for each student

• Materials for an egg drop contest (e.g., paper, tape, popsicle sticks, string, bubble wrap, etc.)

• Prizes for the winner(s) (optional)

Gather together various craft and packaging items for students to use to build a protective shell or container for their eggs. They'll have to work with limited materials and limited time. After they have finished, use a ladder or take the group to a stairwell to drop the eggs. You may choose to reward those contestants whose eggs don't break.

Come back together to brainstorm about what did or didn't work. Ask—

- **How difficult was it to work within the material and time limitations?**
- **What worked? What didn't work?**
- **What would have helped you to protect your egg better—with or without the limitations?**

Now say something like—

Many times we begin working on tasks or problems without having what we need to get the job done. Nehemiah didn't have that issue. He thought through what he needed in order to accomplish his task, and he knew how to go about getting what he needed. 1 Corinthians 14:40 says, "But everything should be done in a fitting and orderly way." Nehemiah was a leader who knew that preparation is the key to motivating people to follow.

IN THE WORD (10 MINUTES)

[ANALYTICAL, AUDITORY]

SETTING

This account takes place in March and April on our calendars. In other words, Nehemiah had been waiting and praying for four months! *(Note: A true leader develops an understanding of the importance of fervent prayer and patiently waiting on God.)*

BACKGROUND

Sanballat, Tobiah, and Geshem were influential rulers in the surrounding areas who wanted to continue their unrestricted access to Jerusalem so they could continue mistreating and cheating the Jews for their own personal gain.

BASIC OUTLINE

I. Preparation for the Task (vv. 1-8)

    A. Proper Timing

        1. The king sees Nehemiah's sadness.

        (Note: Subjects who were sad in the presence of the king were usually killed. Nehemiah had been a good worker and had built a good relationship with the king.)

        2. Nehemiah explains the situation.

        (Note: The end of verse 4 says Nehemiah prayed. We're building from session 1!)

        3. Nehemiah explains his plan to go and strengthen the wall.

        4. The king agrees to send Nehemiah.

        (Note: Nehemiah gives the king a definite time frame and continues with an organized plan. God honors organization—1 Corinthians 14:40.)

    B. Proper Materials

        1. Nehemiah requests some assistance.

            a. He requests letters for traveling.

            b. He requests letters for building materials.

        2. The providence of God is evident.

II. Examination of the Task (vv. 9-16)

A. Personal Protection

(Note: Can you imagine the best of the king's army protecting you? Yet even that mental image is nothing when compared to the providence of God—verse 8.)

B. Thorough Assessment

1. Nehemiah remains silent about what God told him to do.

2. He surveys every part of the wall.

3. He works without anyone else's knowledge.

III. Motivation for the Task (vv. 17-20)

A. Competent in the Situation

1. Nehemiah shows his knowledge of the situation.

(Note: Nehemiah may have been seen as an outsider since he had been away for so long. His silent and thorough assessment was necessary in order to build credibility with the people.)

2. The people agree to follow him.

B. Confident through Opposition

1. There is opposition to the plan.

2. Nehemiah shows his confidence in God's people and plan.

(Note: With God in control, there should be no fear, doubt, or retreat from doing amazing things for him!)

YOU'LL NEED

- Copies of the **Checking Your Walls** repro page (page 29), one for each group
- Pens or pencils

TAKING ANOTHER LOOK (10 MINUTES)

[COMMON SENSE, AUDITORY]

Leaders cannot effectively lead if there are holes or weaknesses in their walls. Have your students get into smaller groups and hand out copies of the **Checking Your Walls** repro page (page 29). Give each group time to answer the questions. When most have finished, ask each group to share a couple of its answers with everyone.

PRACTICAL EXPERIENCE (20 MINUTES)

OPTION 1: LIVING EPITAPH [DYNAMIC, VISUAL]

This activity gives students the opportunity to outline their major life goals and begin to set up strategies for accomplishing them. Give each student a copy of the **Living Epitaph** repro page (page 30). Explain that epitaphs are statements made about someone who has died. This is a time for your students to think through what they would like people to say about them when they are gone and to start living their epitaphs right now. Allow students to work on these individually for 10 to 15 minutes.

Whether they are finished or not, ask your students to share what they've written so far, as well as one or two of their thoughts on the subpoints. It's all right if students don't finish during the allotted time. They can take these sheets home to encourage them to continue thinking about their life goals.

YOU'LL NEED

• Copies of the **Living Epitaph** repro page (page 30), one for each student

• Pens or pencils

OPTION 2: REACHING IN TO REACH OUT [DYNAMIC, VISUAL]

This activity gives students the opportunity to outline their goals for the group and set up strategies for accomplishing those goals. Give each student a copy of the **Reaching in to Reach Out** repro page (page 31). Before having your students work through some more specific goals and ways to accomplish them (and if you've already created a purpose or vision statement for your group), you may wish to begin by reminding them what your group's statement says. If you don't have a vision or purpose statement yet, this activity will help you to develop one with your students.

Take the first 10 to 15 minutes and have your students work on these either individually or in pairs. Whether they are finished or not, ask your students to share their major goals for the group, as well as one or two of their thoughts from the strategy sections. It's okay if students don't finish during the allotted time. They can take these sheets home to encourage them to continue thinking about your youth group's goals.

YOU'LL NEED

• Copies of the **Reaching in to Reach Out** repro page (page 31), one for each student

• Pens or pencils

• Bible

A FINAL WORD (10 MINUTES)

Have a short discussion with your students regarding the following questions:

- **Why is it important to prepare before getting started on a task?**
- **Name some ways in which Nehemiah prepares for his task.**
- **What does his example teach us about what we should do in preparation for our leadership experiences?**
- **Even the "best-laid plans" sometimes don't work out—the results are up to God. How does it make you feel to know that God is ultimately in control?**

- Where did Nehemiah's confidence in God come from?
- How is confidence in God important to leadership?
- How can your preparation motivate those whom you may be leading?
- What are some ways you can prepare to lead those around you?

CLOSING PRAYER

Wrap up your time with a prayer like

God,

We know you honor organization and preparation, and we also know we need to be sure we're prepared to lead others before we can expect them to follow us. However, we can't even begin to lead others until we have first prepared ourselves to be the leaders we need to be. Help us to keep our goals in mind and to line up our lives with your Word and your leading. When we become your true followers, then we can lead others. Help us to strengthen our walls so we can help strengthen those around us.

Amen.

CHECKING YOUR WALLS

Here we see Nehemiah taking time to carefully prepare himself before he looks over the walls of the city in search of flaws or weaknesses that need fixing. In the same way, in order to lead effectively, you must first be sure the wall of protection around your own heart and life is strong enough to stand against opposition.

1. Examine the wall of protection around your heart. What are some of the strengths or weaknesses you see, especially in your relationship with:

   • God?

   • Your family?

   • Those you lead?

2. If opposition came your way right now, how would it affect your life and relationships?

3. If there were opposition to your youth group, how would that affect the members of your group?

4. What could you do to increase the strength of your walls? In your life? In your group?

5. What would you need in order to prepare to lead others?

LIVING EPITAPH

_____

(Your Name)

_____

_____

(How you want to be remembered)

With your epitaph in mind, write down a few thoughts about what might need to change (or what you will continue doing) in the following areas of your life:

- Your relationship with God

- Your relationship with your parents

- Your relationship with your siblings

- Your relationship with your boyfriend or girlfriend

- Your relationship with your future spouse

- Your relationship with your friends

- Your relationships with pastors or spiritual leaders

- Your relationships with those who don't believe in Jesus Christ

WHAT TO DO NOW

1. Begin praying that God will help you to be and do all that he wants for you.
2. Begin working on your relationships in the areas you listed above.
3. Look over this sheet from time to time to see if you can further define any of your thoughts and goals.
4. Start living your life now the way you desire to be remembered in the future. If God put it in your heart, he will help you do it!

REACHING IN TO REACH OUT

There are five basic goals of the church: discipleship, fellowship, ministry, worship, and evangelism. Keeping those in mind, develop a purpose statement for your group (see example below).

Read the Word (discipleship)

Explain God's love (evangelism)

Adore our God (worship)

Connect with believers (fellowship)

Help those around us (ministry)

Acrostics can be a useful and creative way to memorize the purpose of your group. Think through a short statement or one word that summarizes each of the five goals of the church. The sections can be in any order, but be sure to include them all.

YOUR GROUP'S PURPOSE STATEMENT:

Now, under each of those five sections, write out two or three specific goals for your group. Don't be vague in your statements. Make sure each one is practical and measurable (e.g., "Connect with believers—our group will meet every Thursday night for a time of games, testimonies, and sharing").

GROUP GOALS:

1. _____

2. _____

3. _____

4. _____

5. _____

A LEADER INITIATES INCLUSIVENESS

SESSION 3: NEHEMIAH 3

OVERVIEW

The purpose of this session is to encourage students to include everyone in the group they lead.

During this session students will

- Learn to identify ways to encourage people to be involved
- Understand the value of having a sense of ownership of a group or project
- Develop some ways they can be involved and get others involved in their ministries

OPENER (10 MINUTES)

OPTION 1: THE ART OF BALL HANDLING [IMAGINATIVE, KINESTHETIC]

Using cones or masking tape, mark off a square area that is large enough for all of your students to dribble a basketball inside its boundaries. If you have a large group, you may want to divide them into teams of five to six and make several

YOU'LL NEED

- Five or six basketballs

- Cones or masking tape

smaller squares. Have your students step into the square with their basketballs. Tell them they are to dribble around the edge of the square for one minute. If their basketballs are knocked away, then they are out of the game and must exit the square. The winners will be those who are left inside the square when time is up. Students will probably try to knock out the other players' basketballs, but the point of this session is inclusiveness. (Remember: You never *said* to knock out the basketballs! If everyone simply dribbled basketballs in place for one minute, then everyone would win.)

Questions to ask:

- **Why did some (or all) of you try to knock out the other players' basketballs?**
- **What did you really have to do to win?**
- **Could you all have won the game? How?**

Now say something like

Many people feel excluded in groups because of their personalities or their social skills. And they'll feel worse if others really stand out or do better than they do. It's important to discover and make the most of everyone's individual gifts and abilities in order to have a strong group or team. Sometimes the people in your group are just waiting for an opportunity to serve God. They want to follow; they just need a chance. Philippians 2:2 states, "Then make my joy complete by being like-minded, having the same love, being one in spirit and purpose." Even though we're all different, we can put our minds together to accomplish great things for God.

OPTION 2: DRAWING INCLUSIONS (PART 1) [IMAGINATIVE, VISUAL]

YOU'LL NEED

- Sheets of paper, one for each student
- Pencils or pens

Ask your students to recall moments in their lives when someone included them and how that made them feel. Pass out sheets of paper and something to write with. Have your students create a short comic strip of three to four scenes. In their comic strips ask them to sketch the situation in which they were excluded or included, as well as their emotions throughout the situation. When they are finished with their comics, have some volunteers share with the group.

Questions to ask:

- **Why do you think you were excluded in the beginning?**
- **Did you have something to offer the situation? (e.g., Were you a fast runner? Could you play an instrument well? etc.)**
- **How important was it to you to be involved?**

Now say something like

Many people feel excluded in groups because of either their personalities or their social skills. And they'll feel worse if others really stand out or do better than they do.

It's important to discover and make the most of everyone's individual gifts and abilities in order to have a strong group or team. Sometimes the people in your group are just waiting for an opportunity to serve God. They want to follow; they just need a chance. Philippians 2:2 states, "Then make my joy complete by being like-minded, having the same love, being one in spirit and purpose." Even though we're all different, we can put our minds together to accomplish great things for God.

IN THE WORD (10 MINUTES)

[ANALYTICAL, AUDITORY]

AUTHOR

Nehemiah has gone from cupbearer to the head architect and builder. Although he is not mentioned in this passage, the organization and motivation of the people speak highly of his character.

THEME

The theme of this passage really seems to emphasize the people's individual but unified work on the wall. God blessed them as they worked together to accomplish his will for their provision and protection.

BASIC OUTLINE

Though this chapter reads more like a list than a narrative, there are some areas to note along the way:

> I. The priests began the work.
>
> > a. They work on the place of sacrifice.
> >
> > b. This is the only part that was sanctified and prayed over.
>
> II. Some people who don't live in Jerusalem help do the work.
>
> > a. The men of Jericho, Gibeon, and Mizpah
> >
> > b. Zanoah
> >
> > c. Every Israelite takes part in the building of Jerusalem.
> >
> > *(Note: Encourage your students to be more intentional about including those who visit your youth group occasionally or only attend certain social activities. Through constant inclusion, perhaps they will decide to become permanent parts of the group.)*

YOU'LL NEED
• Bibles

III. Some work without the support of their nobility.

    a. The Tekoites make repairs without the nobles' help.

    b. Some people aren't supported by their leaders.

    (Note: Some students' parents or other family members may not support their church involvement.)

IV. Some share in the honor of repairing certain parts of the wall.

    a. Melchizedek, a highly honored and respected high priest, may have been the first to build the old gate.

    b. Jehoiada and Meshullam share the honor of this piece.

V. Leaving behind their trades, they use their skills for one purpose.

    a. Tradesmen didn't mind leaving their jobs to do the work.

    b. They didn't view their jobs as excuses not to do something.

    (Note: Everyone can be involved! Don't stop until you find a way to help.)

VI. They do what is within their reach.

    a. Many work "over against their house."

    b. Some are able to do more than others.

    (Note: We should be concerned with doing our own parts rather than focusing on what others aren't doing.)

VII. The women work with the men.

    a. No gender issues when working for the cause of Christ.

    b. Each has a special place in the work.

VIII. Baruch, works earnestly and may have inspired others to do likewise.

    a. Baruch is an effective and efficient worker.

    b. Some stand out as being excellent workers.

IX. Some do twice the work in order to help the cause.

    a. Meremoth and the Tekoites do extra work.

    b. Some will pick up the slack or help others with their share.

X. Hanun works in spite of what his family did.

    a. Hanun is the sixth son and may have worked in spite of his other five brothers.

    b. Be aware of family stresses in the work.

XI. Nehemiah was an overseer in this passage.

a. We will see more of what he did in chapter 4.

b. Nehemiah allows the people to work according to their skills and abilities and doesn't hoard the responsibility.

(Note: Leaders are supposed to lead, not do all the work themselves. A true leader is not a lone ranger.)

TAKING ANOTHER LOOK (10 MINUTES)

[COMMON SENSE, AUDITORY]

Your students should split off into smaller groups. Hand out copies of the **Different People, Same Mind** repro page (page 39) and something to write with. After they've had some time to answer the questions, have each group share a couple of their answers with everyone.

YOU'LL NEED

- Copies of **Different People, Same Mind** repro page (page 39), one for each group
- Pens or pencils

PRACTICAL EXPERIENCE (20 MINUTES)

OPTION 1: BUILDING WITH LIMITATIONS
[COMMON SENSE, KINESTHETIC]

This activity gives students the opportunity to observe and learn how to work together in spite of their differences. Ahead of time, write the names of various physical handicaps (e.g., only one arm, blind, deaf, and so on) on several slips of paper. Fold the papers and place them in a hat or bowl so your students can each draw one. Ask them not to share the contents of their slips with anyone else.

If you have a large group, you may want to divide students into groups of four or five. Explain to them that they are going to work on a project together while each person acts out his or her assigned physical limitation. Give each group a deck of playing cards and tell them their goal is to build a house of cards—and everyone on the team must participate. Remind them that they will need to figure out the limitations of the others in their groups—without speaking to each other—and then help everyone take part in the project. Give them about 10 minutes to work on their houses. Keep a close watch during the building process to be sure that all the students are participating.

Questions to ask:

- **What was the most difficult part about building your card house?**
- **How would this compare to working with other people when you are in a position of leadership?**
- **What was the key to success in this task?**

YOU'LL NEED

- Slips of paper with a type of physical disability written on each, one for each student
- Hat or container
- Decks of playing cards, one for each small group

YOU'LL NEED

• Paper, one sheet for each student

• Pens or pencils

OPTION 2: DRAWING INCLUSIONS (PART 2) [DYNAMIC, VISUAL]

This activity gives students the opportunity to think through how they can include others—whatever their skills or abilities. It will help them visualize (in their minds and with their hands) how they can influence others and encourage them in their ministry for Christ.

Ask students to think of some realistic future situations in which they could help others feel included in their group. Pass out sheets of paper and have students create a short comic strip containing three to four scenes. In their comic strips ask them to draw what it would look like to be excluded or included and the emotions felt throughout the scenario. Ask them to include themselves in their drawings and focus on how they can be inclusive of those around them. When they are finished, have some volunteers share their drawings with the group. If you have a place to display these comics, it may be good to do so as a future reminder of the importance of including others.

A FINAL WORD (10 MINUTES)

Have a short discussion with your students and ask the following questions:

- **Why is it important to include every member of your group—especially visitors?**
- **What are some of the skills of the people in chapter 3 of Nehemiah that added to the building of the wall?**
- **How can you learn more about the abilities of the people in your group?**
- **What are some ways you can include members of your group in planning and future projects?**
- **Why is it so hard for some leaders to delegate tasks and authority? Is it hard for you? Explain.**

CLOSING PRAYER

Wrap up your time with a prayer like

God,

You made each one of us special and unique. We can each contribute to your work in our own way, but some of us need encouragement and the opportunity to serve. As we lead others, we can't focus on our differences. Instead we need to focus on obeying you and using our differences to work together for your glory. Please help us to do just that.

Amen.

DIFFERENT PEOPLE, SAME MIND

In chapter 3, Nehemiah is not in the spotlight. Instead, we get to see the involvement of the builders and their special skills. Likewise, each person in our group has something unique and of great benefit to contribute to the work we do for God. Consider your part in making sure that, like Nehemiah, you include everyone.

1. Should one person do all the work? Why or why not?

2. Will everyone encourage the work?

3. Does everyone have an important part in the work?

4. What brings outsiders in to help with the work?

5. What does involvement have to do with ownership? Why is ownership important?

6. If everyone were not involved, how would things be different?

7. What is the job of the person or leader who started the work?

A LEADER DEALS WITH DISTRACTIONS

OVERVIEW

The purpose of this session is to help students learn to deal with distractions.

During this session students will

- Learn to identify various types of distractions
- Understand how they should respond to distractions
- Develop proactive plans to respond appropriately

OPENER (10 MINUTES)

OPTION 1: DAILY DISTRACTIONS [IMAGINATIVE, KINESTHETIC]

Make a copy of the **Daily Distractions Role Play** page (page 46) and cut out the strips for each role. Choose four students from your group to act out a scene that takes place in a home. The first student will be trying to do his daily quiet times, but it won't be easy. Give the actors three or four minutes to complete the scene.

> **YOU'LL NEED**
>
> • A copy of the **Daily Distractions Role Play** page (page 46), cut apart

After the role-play ends, ask—

- **What types of distractions did the first student encounter?**
- **Have you ever experienced any of those distractions before?**
- **How can you make your quiet time a priority with all of those distractions?**

Now say something like

In our role play, the distractions were not necessarily bad things, but they were distractions nonetheless. Nehemiah also experienced some distractions, but they weren't as minor as what we experience on a typical day. Leaders need to keep their focus on God. As Hebrews 12:2 states, "Let us fix our eyes on Jesus, the author and perfecter of our faith, who for the joy set before him endured the cross, scorning its shame, and sat down at the right hand of the throne of God." Whether good or bad, Nehemiah knew how to deal with distractions and faithfully finish the job.

YOU'LL NEED

- Overhead or PowerPoint® image of the **Word Jumble** repro sheet (page 47)

- Overhead or PowerPoint projector

OPTION 2: WORD JUMBLE [IMAGINATIVE, VISUAL]

Ahead of time, copy Part 1 of the **Word Jumble** repro page (page 47) onto an overhead transparency or PowerPoint slide. Project it and give your students some time to look it over. Let them know that a key verse is hidden among the words. They can work in pairs or groups and may talk out loud to figure it out.

If they get stuck, you can give them a clue about the pattern used to hide the words of this verse (i.e., a key word appears every four words). If they're still stuck, you can project an image of Part 2 from the **Word Jumble** repro page, where the key words are boldfaced within the paragraph. And if that doesn't help, just tell them it's from Nehemiah 4:6 (NASB)—"For the people had a mind to work."

Questions to ask afterward:

- **What types of distractions did you experience when trying to locate the key verse?**
- **What helped or could have helped you figure it out?**
- **What does the verse tell you happened in the midst of the distractions?**

Now say something like

In our Word Jumble there was a pattern for finding the words in our key verse. But God has already given us a pattern to follow in his living Word. Nehemiah knew exactly what God wanted, and he wasn't going to let anything distract him. Leaders need to keep their focus on God. As Hebrews 12:2 states, "Let us fix our eyes on Jesus, the author and perfecter of our faith, who for the joy set before him endured the cross, scorning its shame, and sat down at the right hand of the throne of God." Whether good or bad, Nehemiah knew how to deal with distractions and faithfully finish the job.

IN THE WORD (10 MINUTES)

[ANALYTICAL, AUDITORY]

PEOPLE

Sanballat—a Moabite, or descendant of Lot's son, Moab, whose tribe had a long-running history of dislike and violence with the Israelites. (The book of Ruth is written about King David's great-grandmother Ruth, another member of this tribe.) Sanballat had made business arrangements with the people of Jerusalem and did not like being cut off from his plundering.

Tobiah—an Ammonite, or descendant of Lot's son, Ben-Ammi, is in a tribe closely linked to the Moabites and therefore also historically opposed to the Israelites. Tobiah has strong connections with those who are rebuilding the wall—he is the son-in-law of Shechaniah, and Tobiah's son married a Jewish woman.

BASIC OUTLINE

I. The Scorning Crowd (vv. 1-3)

    A. Sanballat is angry about the progress.

        1. He gathers the enemies of Israel together.

        2. He questions the purpose of God's people.

    B. Tobiah responds with sarcasm and believes they will never make a go of it.

II. A Determined People (vv. 4-6)

    A. Nehemiah prays for God to deal with the enemy.

    (Note: Prayer has been a key from the very start.)

    B. The people are able to remain focused so they can continue building.

III. The Conspiring Crowd (vv. 7-8)

    A. Sanballat and his friends become angry.

    B. They begin to make plans to go to war.

IV. A Focused People (vv. 9-14)

    A. Nehemiah prays again.

    B. The people prepare a defense.

    (Note: Nehemiah listens to their thoughts and concerns and then acts on them. A true leader is also an excellent listener.)

    C. Nehemiah reminds the people of God's great power.

V. A United People (vv. 15-23)

> A. The enemy backs off when Nehemiah and the people are prepared to fight.

> B. Half of Nehemiah's servants build, and the other half stay ready to defend.

> C. The Jews build with one hand and hold a weapon in the other hand.

> *(Note: The people did not stop building the wall. They stayed focused despite the distractions—thanks to a strong, focused leader.)*

> D. Nehemiah keeps the people prepared in case of attack.

TAKING ANOTHER LOOK (10 MINUTES)

OPTION 1: DISTRACTED OR NOT DISTRACTED? [COMMON SENSE, AUDITORY]

YOU'LL NEED

• Copies of **Distracted or Not Distracted?** repro page (page 48), one for each group

• Pens or pencils

• Bibles

Have your students get into small groups and hand each a copy of the **Distracted or Not Distracted?** repro page (page 48) and a Bible. Give the groups time to answer the questions. When most have finished, ask the groups to share a couple of their answers with everyone.

OPTION 2: NUMBER PROBLEMS [COMMON SENSE, VISUAL]

YOU'LL NEED

• *A Beautiful Mind* DVD (Universal Pictures, 2001)

• TV and DVD player

Start 00:24:50 Aerial view of the Pentagon, 1953.

Stop 00:28:05 Dr. Nash (Russell Crowe) is escorted from the room

In this scene Dr. John Nash (Russell Crowe) is working as an analyst at Wheeler Defense Labs during the Cold War. A United States army general has asked Nash to help them crack a numerical code that was intercepted from some Russian radio transmissions. Once the situation has been explained to him, Nash immediately begins to work on the problem and keeps his focus trained on the numbers until he ultimately deciphers what the code means and explains it to the general and his aides.

Questions to ask:

* **What were the distractions that fought for Nash's attention in this scene?**
* **How does he respond?**
* **When he breaks the code, what finally gives it away?**

Now say something like

In Nehemiah 4, the focus is on building the wall. That focus has never changed since chapter 1. Nehemiah did not have to search for a pattern or focus; God gave it to him. God's plan of provision for and protection of his people was laid out in the very

beginning, and it never would have happened if Nehemiah and the builders had not dealt with the distractions. We also need to develop some ways to prepare ourselves for when distractions try to keep us from doing what God wants.

PRACTICAL EXPERIENCE (20 MINUTES)

[DYNAMIC, KINESTHETIC]

YOU'LL NEED

• A variety of props (optional)

This activity gives students the opportunity to practice what they've been learning and begin thinking about how they will remain focused and resolved on a daily basis. Divide your students into groups. Give each group time to come up with a particular situation where a distraction keeps a person from doing what God wants her to do. Then they should develop a short skit that portrays how that person can appropriately respond to distractions and continue keeping her focus on the goal ahead. Have students perform their scenes for the rest of the group. After each one, take time to discuss what was good about the response they portrayed, as well as other possible responses.

A FINAL WORD (10 MINUTES)

Have a short discussion with your students using the following questions to get you started:

* **Why is it important to know how to deal with distractions?**
* **What does Nehemiah's example teach us about dealing with distractions?**
* **How can you prepare for future distractions in your life?**
* **What kind of listener are you?**
* **How can listening to others help or hinder your ability to lead them?**
* **Using what we've learned in this session, what are some ways you could help others deal with the distractions in their lives?**

CLOSING PRAYER

Wrap up your time with a prayer like

God,

In order to lead effectively, we need to know how to respond appropriately to distractions. People will be looking to us as examples of how they should respond. If we don't deal with distractions correctly, our goals may never be accomplished. Help us persevere through the distractions and finish well for ourselves, for others, and for the cause of Christ. Amen.

DAILY DISTRACTIONS ROLE PLAY

Cut out the following descriptions and distribute them to a few of your students at the beginning of the session.

✂ ---

Student #1—You are trying to find time throughout the day to do your daily devotions. When friends try to get you to do things with them, you work out another time to do your devotions and go with your friends instead. When you're finished, come back and do your devotions.

✂ ---

Student #2—Student #1 is your sibling. Before you speak, announce that it is 3 p.m. Then ask Student #1 to help you with your homework for a few minutes. Later, you'll enter the room a second time (after Student #1 returns from going out with friends). Announce that it's 9 p.m. and time for your favorite TV show.

✂ ---

Student #3—Student #1 is your child. Before you speak, announce that it is 5 p.m. Then come in and tell Student #1 that it's time to do some chores and then wash up for dinner. Come in a second time (after the TV show ends), announce that it's 10 p.m., and then tell Student #1 to get ready for bed.

✂ ---

Student #4—Student #1 is your friend. Before you speak, announce that it's 6:30 p.m. Call and invite Student #1 to go out with you for a couple hours. Promise to get Student #1 back home soon.

WORD JUMBLE

PART 1

Have toward despised for land sword God the therefore rulers rest people indignation Jews places had rose said nobles a unto builders wall mind bearers known pass to Sanballat lower counsel work cease families fight.

PART 2

Have toward despised **for** land sword God **the** therefore rulers rest **people** indignation Jews places **had** rose said nobles **a** unto builders wall **mind** bearers known pass **to** Sanballat lower counsel **work** cease families fight.

DISTRACTED OR NOT DISTRACTED?

1. In what ways do the enemies of the Jews try to attack or distract Nehemiah?

2. Have you ever been distracted from accomplishing your goals? If so, explain.

3. How did you respond to these distractions?

4. How does Nehemiah respond to his enemies?

5. List some possible distractions that might keep you from following God.

6. In light of Nehemiah's example, what are some ways you can prepare for distractions like these?

7. Why is it important for leaders to know how to deal with distractions?

8. How will the way you respond affect those you might lead?

A LEADER INSTILLS INTEGRITY

OVERVIEW

This session is designed to introduce the importance of integrity in a leadership role.

During this session students will

- Learn to identify sinful practices
- Understand how to correct them
- Practice being people of integrity

OPENER (10 MINUTES)

OPTION 1: PIPE CLEANING HOUSE
[IMAGINATIVE, KINESTHETIC]

At times, we all need to clean house. There are things in our lives that need work in order to keep us pure and available for God's use. In this activity, give each student four to five pipe cleaners. Ask them to create objects that represent some of the things that keep them from being all they can be for God. When they are finished, have some volunteers share their creations with the rest of the group.

YOU'LL NEED

- Four or five pipe cleaners for each student

Ask—

- **How do these things keep us from being godly leaders?**
- **How could these things affect the people around us?**
- **What are some ways we can go about correcting these things in the days ahead?**

Now say something like

People look to their leaders for the standards by which they live their lives. If leaders aren't pulling their weight, then why should the people who are following them do any better? Nehemiah had to be a strong example of integrity in order to keep the people in tune with what God wanted them to do. We all need to make sure our hearts and motives are in the right place. David asks God in Psalm 139:23-24, "Search me, O God, and know my heart; test me and know my anxious thoughts. See if there is any offensive way in me, and lead me in the way everlasting." Leaders must be people of high integrity.

OPTION 2: THE GREAT DISCONNECT [IMAGINATIVE, VISUAL]

Before your group time, take some small pieces of paper and write on each one a sin that might keep your students from living lives of integrity. Remove the lamp from the flashlight and place the small pieces of paper in between the battery and the lamp. When you are ready to begin the session, talk about how leaders are lights for others to follow and switch on the flashlight. *(Note: It obviously won't work.)*

Questions to ask:

- **What would keep the flashlight from working?** *(The Holy Spirit is the power source in our lives. And having no batteries could cause the flashlight not to work. But there are batteries inside the flashlight, and they are installed correctly. Now open the flashlight to show the batteries to your students and "discover" the papers inside.)*
- **Could these thin little papers keep the flashlight from working?** *(Thin as they may be, the sins written on these little papers disconnect us from the power of God to lead lives of integrity. Discuss the items you have written on the papers and how they could disconnect us from God.)*
- **Can I leave just one paper** *(sin)* **that I don't want to deal with right now and still get the flashlight to work?** *(No. Take out all the papers, reconnect the lamp to the power source, and shine the light around the room.)*

Now say something like

We might consider our sins and distractions small, but they are huge when we consider the effect they have on our light as leaders of integrity. We need to consider the level of integrity we show and *should* show as leaders. Nehemiah had to be a strong example of integrity in order to keep the people in tune with what God wanted them to do. We

all need to make sure our hearts and motives are in the right place. David asks God in Psalm 139:23-24, "Search me, O God, and know my heart; test me and know my anxious thoughts. See if there is any offensive way in me, and lead me in the way everlasting." Leaders must be people of high integrity.

IN THE WORD (10 MINUTES)

[ANALYTICAL, AUDITORY]

AUTHOR

In this passage, Nehemiah moves from the position of chief architect to governor.

BACKGROUND

Nehemiah finds the people doing several things that are against the Mosaic Law:

- Slavery—a Hebrew slave should only serve six years and then be freed on the seventh (Exodus 21:2-11). This would be in accordance with the Year of Jubilee (Leviticus 25).
- Interest on Loans—the Hebrew people were never to charge interest on loans made to other Hebrews (Exodus 22:25).
- Selling Slaves—they were never to sell people to pay off debts or for any other reason. God brought them out of slavery in Egypt and would not tolerate having this practice continue among the Hebrew people (Leviticus 25:42).

In the culture of the day, shaking out the folds of your robe (Nehemiah 5:13) was a visual rejection of any who might violate the agreement set forth.

BASIC OUTLINE

I. Charging the People (vv. 1-6)

   A. Lack of Necessities

   (Note: There is a famine in the land.)

   B. Borrowing to Pay Debt

   (Note: They have trouble paying King Artaxerxes' taxes. Also, their creditors are charging interest on borrowed funds.)

   C. Slavery to Pay Debt

   (Note: Both the interest charges and the practice of slavery are against Mosaic Law, and this is why Nehemiah becomes angry.)

II. Chastening the Practice (vv. 7-13)

    A. Confronting the Problem

    (Note: A good leader always goes to the source of the problem and always thinks before speaking. Also, Nehemiah never would have been able to confront the people if he were not a person of proven character and integrity.)

    B. Comparison to the Enemy

    C. Commitment to the Change

        1. Immediately corrects the situation.

        2. Makes a public commitment to God.

III. Changing the Position (vv. 14-19)

    A. The Selfish Rulers

    (Note: Previous governors used tax money for personal gain and parties.)

    B. The Godly Ruler

    (Note: Nehemiah, the new governor, gets his hands dirty working with the people, and he never uses the city's money for his own personal gain. A godly leader works with the people and puts their needs before his own desires.)

TAKING ANOTHER LOOK (15 MINUTES)

[COMMON SENSE, AUDITORY]

Have your students get into small groups and hand each a copy of the **What Would You Do?** repro page (page 55) and something to write with. Give them time to answer the questions. When most of them have finished, have each group share a couple of their answers with the rest of the group.

PRACTICAL EXPERIENCE (20 MINUTES)

OPTION 1: A LEADER'S LIFE [DYNAMIC, AUDITORY]

This activity not only has students personally reflect on their lives, but it also provides a form of accountability that is crucial to maintaining lives of integrity. Listen to the song "This Is Your Life" on Switchfoot's *The Beautiful Letdown* album. Have students take time to think about how they can specifically work on the areas of their lives that are keeping them from being leaders of high integrity.

YOU'LL NEED

• Copies of the **What Would You Do?** repro page (page 55), one for each student

• Pencils or pens

YOU'LL NEED

• A copy of Switchfoot's *The Beautiful Letdown* album (Sparrow/ Columbia, 2003)

• CD player

• Sheets of paper, one for each student

• Envelopes, one for each student

• Pencils or pens

Pass out sheets of paper, pencils or pens, and envelopes. Ask your students to write a personal letter stating how they will begin working on those areas over the next four weeks. When they are finished, have them put the letters in the envelopes and seal them. You can collect these and let your students know you will be giving them back in four weeks as checks on their progress.

OPTION 2: MIRROR, MIRROR OF THE WORD [DYNAMIC, KINESTHETIC]

This activity not only asks students to personally reflect on their lives in the mirror of God's Word, but it also provides a form of accountability that is crucial to maintaining a life of integrity.

Let your students know that they have two options:

1. They can find a verse of Scripture that applies directly to the area(s) on which they will be working. Then ask them to draw pictures or comics of the verse, which they can display in a highly visible place at home or in their school lockers.
2. They can write out scenarios or purpose statements of how to live out a verse of Scripture they find, or they can use Philippians 4:8-9 as their foundation.

They will need to leave space at the bottom of each of these options to have accountability partners (godly family members or friends) who will check in with them from time to time to see how they are doing and sign their sheets. Collect their statements and let your students know they will revisit these in one month to see how they are doing. (You may need to make copies for them to take home with them.)

A FINAL WORD (10 MINUTES)

Have a short discussion with your students and ask the following questions:

* **Why is it important to be a leader of integrity?**
* **What does Nehemiah's example teach us about integrity?**
* **Do you believe that others view you as being a person of integrity? How do you know?**
* **How do you feel when you witness an obvious lack of integrity in others' actions? Explain.**
* **Describe how you confront a problem. How do the other parties respond when you confront them?**
* **How are you preparing yourselves to have integrity as you lead others now or in the future?**
* **What are some specific ways that you can help others live lives of integrity?**

CLOSING PRAYER

Wrap up your time with a prayer like

God,

We know that leaders need to be people of integrity—they set the standard for all who follow them. "Little" lies and sins can keep us from accomplishing your plans for us. We need to regularly examine our hearts and lives, as well as be accountable to people we trust in order to keep our lives in line with the mirror of your Word. Please help us to set a high standard of integrity for ourselves and for those who may be looking to us as their leaders.

Amen.

WHAT WOULD YOU DO?

Consider the following scenarios in your groups and share your answers with the rest of the group.

1. What would you do if you walked out of a store with something in your hand that you forgot to pay for?

2. What would you do if you missed the trash can on your way out of a bathroom?

3. What would you do if you saw a friend breaking a rule at school?

4. What would you do if someone gossiped to you?

5. What would you do if a friend told you she was hurting herself physically but you shouldn't tell anyone else about it?

A LEADER REMAINS RESOLVED

SESSION 6: NEHEMIAH 6

OVERVIEW

The purpose of this session is to underscore the importance of resolve in the life of a leader.

During this session students will

- Be able to identify the importance of staying resolved
- Understand how to respond to persecution
- Become steadfast in their pursuit of God

OPENER (10 MINUTES)

[IMAGINATIVE, KINESTHETIC]

Create your own obstacle course. Take one student aside and blindfold him. Have another student stand to the side and try to take the blindfolded student through the course. There's one catch, though—the other students are at liberty to scream, move anywhere about the course, and try to misdirect the blindfolded student (or whatever it takes to be a distraction and get the blindfolded student to run into an obstacle). However, no one is allowed to touch the blindfolded student running the course. Once the student touches an obstacle or reaches the end of the course, the illustration ends.

Questions to ask:

- **We should know how to deal with distractions from our session in Nehemiah 4. Does having that knowledge make it any easier in a situation like this?**
- **Was it difficult to focus on the person giving the good directions?**
- **How might it have been easier to receive direction from that person?**

Now say something like

Not only does a leader need to know how to deal with distractions, but she also needs to have a strong sense of resolve in order to continue the work and keep the focus on God. Even though the distractions continued and persecution increased, Nehemiah was resolved to finish the work God had called him to do. We need to remain resolved and keep our minds on 1 John 4:4—"You, dear children, are from God and have overcome them, because the one who is in you is greater than the one who is in the world." A resolved leader has a God-perspective on life that keeps others focused on God's will, too.

IN THE WORD (10 MINUTES)

[ANALYTICAL, AUDITORY]

PEOPLE

Shemaiah—a false prophet living in Jerusalem. Tobiah and Sanballat hired him, and his name is typically used by the Levites. He could have been a respected leader in Jerusalem at the time.

BASIC OUTLINE

I. A Crafty Approach (vv. 1-4)

(Note: The enemy attacks again right before the construction is completed, and they finally lose control of the people living inside the walls once and for all.)

A. The enemy tries to get Nehemiah alone so they can trap him.

(Note: The enemy does not give up—they try four more times! Yet Nehemiah remains resolved.)

B. Nehemiah remains focused and resolves to continue doing God's work.

(Note: Remember the principle from Nehemiah 4—he wasn't willing to let the work stop for any reason.)

II. A False Accusation (vv. 5-9)

A. Sanballat accuses Nehemiah of leading the Jews to rebel against King Artaxerxes (Nehemiah's boss) and to make Nehemiah their king.

(Note: Notice the enemy attacks his integrity right after Nehemiah confronted the people with this issue in the previous chapter.)

B. Nehemiah exposes the lie and goes right to God to ask for the strength to remain resolved through the difficult time.

(Note: Remember where we started in Nehemiah—on our knees!)

III. A Lying Acquaintance (vv. 10-14)

A. Shemaiah wants Nehemiah to use the temple as a refuge where they can discuss what is going on—and so Shemaiah can discourage Nehemiah.

(Note: Sometimes the enemy can be in your own camp.)

B. Nehemiah recognizes his position under the guidance and direction of God and refuses to flee.

(Note: Nehemiah knows that God protects his leaders; Nehemiah also relies on insight and discernment from the Holy Spirit.)

IV. A Great Accomplishment (vv. 15-19)

A. The people complete the work in an amazing time frame.

(Note: It only took them 52 days to complete the wall! This would not have been possible had it not been for a leader who was resolved. It was an all-inclusive victory that brought glory to God, even in the sight of the enemy.)

B. The enemy continues to try to bring Nehemiah down—both inside and outside the walls—even after the work has been completed.

(Note: "Completed" refers to the work on the wall. The job was only half-done in Nehemiah's eyes.)

TAKING ANOTHER LOOK (15 MINUTES)

OPTION 1: TESTING YOUR RESOLVE
[COMMON SENSE, AUDITORY]

Have your students divide into small groups and hand each a copy of the **Testing Your Resolve** repro page (page 62), something to write with, and a Bible. Give the groups time to answer the questions. When most have finished, ask each group to share a couple of its answers with everyone.

YOU'LL NEED
- Copies of the **Testing Your Resolve** repro page (page 62), one for each small group
- Pencils or pens
- Bibles

YOU'LL NEED

• *A Knight's Tale* DVD (Columbia Pictures, 2001)

• TV and DVD player

OPTION 2: STANDING ALONE [COMMON SENSE, VISUAL]

Start 01:43:55 Sir William (Heath Ledger) says, "Alive! Can you imagine?"

Stop 01:48:30 Sir William's squire, Roland (Mark Addy), says, "Let's end them together."

Sir William (Heath Ledger) was born a peasant during a period of history when your lineage was everything—it could make or break your future. William had always wanted to be a knight, so when he sees an opportunity to live out his fantasy, he pretends to be a royal knight and enters jousting contests using a false name and forged papers. William and his friends know that if the truth is ever discovered, the penalty for such deceit will be very serious. In this scene, William's herald, Geoffrey (Paul Bettany), tells William that he is about to be arrested for impersonating a knight, and then Geoffrey and the rest of William's friends try to convince him to run away and avoid the inevitable trip to the stocks.

Questions to ask:

- **Why didn't Sir William run when he had the chance?**
- **How do you think he felt while listening to what his friends were saying?**
- **What might you have done in this situation?**

Now say something like

You know your enemies will be after you to keep you from reaching your goals, but sometimes your friends won't be very encouraging, either. Sometimes, just like Nehemiah, even those you work with and trust will try to get you to quit. You can't let even the closest and strongest of discouragements or persecutions keep you from following what you know to be right according to God's plan for you. Stay resolved to do the work, knowing that God will be with you every step of the way.

PRACTICAL EXPERIENCE (20 MINUTES)

[DYNAMIC, KINESTHETIC]

YOU'LL NEED

• Paper and pencils for each small group

This activity will give students opportunities to regularly reach out to those around them on a specific and individual basis. This will open communication between leaders and other students for developing encouraging and effective ministry experiences.

Attacks can very easily lead to discouragement. It is important for leaders to be motivators and encouragers of their people and to remain resolved to the task. Considering the discussions and thoughts that came up during the last activity, have your students get together in groups of three or four to work on ways to consistently encourage members of the youth group (or whatever group they may be leading) and remind them of God's blessings and plans for their lives. Each group should work on a plan, decide how it will be carried out, and prepare to present those plans to the rest of the group. As they share their ideas, keep track of them all for future reference, but have the groups agree on one that could be put into action right away.

A FINAL WORD (10 MINUTES)

Have a short discussion with your students and ask the following questions:

- **Which situation would be more difficult for you—standing up to an enemy from outside the walls of your personal life (such as an acquaintance or a stranger) or facing an enemy from within (such as a close friend or family member)? Explain your answer.**
- **Can you think of a time when someone attacked your integrity (e.g., falsely accused you of lying or cheating)? What happened? How did you feel when these things were said about you?**
- **Why is resolve necessary in the life of a leader?**
- **How did Nehemiah maintain his sense of resolve as the workers finished the construction of the wall?**
- **Describe a time when something so amazing happened that you knew God was the one who did it (e.g., Nehemiah and his crew finished rebuilding the wall in only 52 days despite all of the obstacles and setbacks that their enemies threw their way).**
- **What are some things you can do to be more resolved?**
- **What are some specific ways your resolve will help others for the cause of Christ?**

CLOSING PRAYER

Wrap up your time with a prayer like

God,

Resolve is a necessity in the life of a leader. Otherwise people might get discouraged, and the work would not be completed. People are looking for leaders with strong foundations of unwavering truth that guide and direct their lives. Leaders with minds that see life within your power and protection can be confident in the tasks you give them. We need to be praying that our focus and our perception of the things around us will always keep your power and will in our minds. Then we can be leaders who are resolved to complete the ministries you have prepared for each and every one of us.

Amen.

TESTING YOUR RESOLVE

Nehemiah has some difficult things to deal with in chapter 6. How he responds to the attacks and lies is key to his resolve in completing the task God gives him to do. We would do well to take another look at his responses and see how we might imitate those in our own lives. Strong leaders need to be able to remain resolved in the midst of difficult times.

1. In what ways did the enemies of the Jews try to attack Nehemiah?

2. How did Nehemiah respond to each attack?

3. What was the key to Nehemiah's ability to stay resolved to finish the wall?

4. How can you prepare yourself ahead of time to strengthen your resolve for the attacks that may come in the days ahead?

5. How will your responses affect those around you, especially the people you may be leading right now?

A LEADER ACTIVELY ADMINISTRATES

OVERVIEW

The purpose of this session is to teach students to be effective administrators.

During this session students will

- Learn to identify the needs of their group
- Understand how to effectively organize their group
- Practice their skills by planning an event

OPENER (10 MINUTES)

OPTION 1: ORGANIZING THE TROOPS [IMAGINATIVE, VISUAL]

Start 00:23:41 Samuel Gerard (Tommy Lee Jones) says, "Listen up, ladies and gentlemen!"

Stop 00:24:20 Gerard says, "Go get him."

Dr. Richard Kimble (Harrison Ford) was sent to jail for killing his wife—a crime he says he didn't commit. Right before this scene, the prison bus that was transporting Kimble and some of his fellow inmates collided with a moving train. Richard and another inmate survived and fled on foot. When Deputy U.S. Marshal Samuel Gerard (Tommy Lee Jones) and his team arrive at the scene of the accident, they take over the investigation, and Gerard quickly organizes his crew to start the search.

Questions to ask:

- What did the U.S. marshals do first?
- Why was it important for Gerard to know the area?
- How did he make sure all the bases were covered?

Now say something like

A leader needs to know the needs and abilities of her people. From there she can best determine how to make things happen. Nehemiah knew the land, the needs, and his people. God put it in his heart to make sure things were completely organized and legitimate in order to finish the job in Jerusalem. Had he not done this, the walls might once again have come crashing down due to the weaknesses of the people and their leadership. First Corinthians 14:40 says, "But everything should be done in a fitting and orderly way." Nehemiah was actively involved in administration and organization.

OPTION 2: DRY RUN REVIEW [IMAGINATIVE, KINESTHETIC]

Ahead of time, search for as many markers or pens you can find that are out of or almost out of ink and put them together in a container. Now set out your box or basket full of markers or pens and make sure each student has a piece of paper. Tell your students that you will be reviewing the first half of the study. Ask them to choose a marker or pen and write down the titles or leadership principles from the first six sessions. The first student to turn in a complete and correct list gets a prize.

As your students go through the markers and pens, they will have a difficult time writing out the principles. Of course, you can stick in one or two writing utensils that do contain ink so someone can finish the list! When it's over, take some time to review the principles and then discuss the activity.

Questions to ask:

- **Why did so many of you have a hard time writing out the review?**
- **Is it enough to just have a bunch of markers or pens collected together? Is it enough that they look the same on the outside?**
- **How could you avoid having something like this happen in the future?**

YOU'LL NEED
- Container full of nearly dried-out markers or pens with low ink
- Sheets of paper, one for each student
- Prize for the contest winner

Now say something like

Sometimes people look fine on the outside, but they are not doing well on the inside. It is important that leaders who actively administrate appoint godly leaders to serve under them. In Nehemiah's case, he doesn't exclude people from the task of rebuilding the wall; he only excludes them from leadership. Impure leadership can and will corrupt what you are trying to do for God. Nehemiah wouldn't have known what was what if he hadn't taken a record of the people. First Corinthians 14:40 states, "But everything should be done in a fitting and orderly way." Nehemiah was actively involved in administration and organization.

IN THE WORD (10 MINUTES)

[ANALYTICAL, AUDITORY]

PEOPLE

YOU'LL NEED
- Bibles

The role of priest was reserved for those in the Levitical line (Numbers 3:6). During this time some who were trying to be priests could not prove their connection. Although the reason is unknown, it could be that these people were trying to become priests during this time of famine in order to guarantee food and care. In order to preserve the integrity and purity of the people and spiritual leaders, this could not be allowed.

BASIC OUTLINE

I. Develops Potential (vv. 1-4)

    A. Recognizes leadership

    (Note: Keys to look for: faithfulness and fear of God.)

    B. Delegates responsibility

    (Note: Each family had leadership over the areas near their homes to protect and build.)

II. Organizes Families (vv. 5-60)

    A. Led by God to make a record according to genealogy

    (Note: God is in favor of good organization and administration.)

    B. Records those who were of Israel

III. Defends Purity (vv. 61-65)

(Note: Instilling integrity is a continuous process.)

A. Discovers many who could not prove their connection to the tribe of Levi.

B. Does not allow them to be involved in the role of priest.

(Note: He does not keep them from being involved altogether, but it is important to make the distinction between the priests and the regular workers.)

IV. Oversees Funding (vv. 66-73)

A. The people contributed through servants and work animals.

B. Some gave money for the effort and took care of the priests.

(Note: There are many ways that people can help. Don't look down on even the smallest contributions.)

YOU'LL NEED

• Copies of the **Setting the Record Straight** repro page (page 69), one for each student

• Pencils or pens

• Bibles

YOU'LL NEED

• A simple organizational chart of your church or another group

TAKING ANOTHER LOOK (15 MINUTES)

OPTION 1: SETTING THE RECORD STRAIGHT [COMMON SENSE, AUDITORY]

Have your students get into small groups. Hand each a copy of the **Setting the Record Straight** repro page (page 69), something to write with, and a Bible. Give each group time to answer the questions. When most of the groups have finished, ask each to share a couple of its answers with the rest of the group.

OPTION 2: ORGANIZING LEADERSHIP [COMMON SENSE, VISUAL]

Prepare a simplified chart of the leadership positions in your church or group and provide a description of how they each care for the needs of the people (e.g., Senior Pastor – Pastoral Staff – Deacons – Congregation). Explain to your students how keeping the volunteers and leaders organized ensures that the needs of the people are being met by the ministries of your church or group.

Questions to ask:

* **Looking at this chart, what are some of the areas where we are or should be the strongest?**
* **What are some areas where we might need to improve?**
* **How could you help in those areas?**
* **How could you use something like this to lead our group?**

Now say something like

Organization and godly leadership are important to the growth of your ministry for Christ, as well as to making sure the needs of the people you lead are being met.

We should always be evaluating our organizational skills to see what areas we can improve along the way.

PRACTICAL EXPERIENCE (20 MINUTES)

[DYNAMIC, AUDITORY]

YOU'LL NEED
• Sheets of paper for each group
• Pencils or pens

If you have a smaller group, have your students stay together for this activity. If you have a larger group, you may want to divide them into groups of six to eight. In their groups, the students will be planning a fundraising event. If your group will be taking a mission trip soon, this would be a good motivator. If not, you may want to research some possibilities of people in your church with financial needs, a community ministry to which you could donate funds, or a missionary you could help.

Whatever you decide, have your students do the organizing and planning with only minimal input from you. Let them appoint a leader or chairperson for the committee, delegate responsibility to other members, and work with you to schedule the event (e.g., if they decide to do a car wash, they need to figure out who will bring the supplies, who will secure the location, who will take care of promoting the event, who will handle funds that are raised, and so on).

Before your students leave, make sure they have scheduled their next meeting time to do some further planning and receive updates from committee members about their assigned tasks. This will be a great opportunity for your students to practice actively administrating while promoting a tremendous missions ministry from your church or organization.

A FINAL WORD (10 MINUTES)

Have a short discussion with your students and ask the following questions:

* **Why is it important to be and stay organized?**
* **What did Nehemiah see as important during the organization process?**
* **What are some ways you could be more organized and actively administrating things in your life?**
* **How could your active administration influence the lives of people in your group, church, community, and around the world?**
* **What are some ways you could identify the abilities of others in your group?**
* **What do you think is the most difficult part of planning a group event? What steps can you take to make it easier?**

CLOSING PRAYER

Wrap up your time with a prayer like

God,

Organization and administration are not always fun tasks. However, we know you bless these efforts and can multiply the ministries we have been called to do. Leaders who keep things in order, defend purity, and maintain individual and group integrity can do amazing things for the cause of Christ. Help us to be active administrators for his glory.

Amen.

SETTING THE RECORD STRAIGHT

The people had a wall. Now they needed some leadership and organization to make sure things didn't fall apart again. Nehemiah recognized these needs and took action. The principles he followed are good to keep in mind as we organize those around us to do great things for Jesus Christ.

1. What did Nehemiah observe in those he put into leadership?

2. What was Nehemiah's major endeavor after setting up the leadership?

3. Why is recordkeeping important? How does that affect purity? How does that affect the funding of the effort?

4. What could you do now to benefit future endeavors through recordkeeping?

5. What are important traits for you to develop as a leader according to this passage?

OVERVIEW

The focus of this session is to instill in students the importance of teaching the truth of God's Word.

During this session students will

- Learn to identify the need for truth
- Understand how to present biblical truth
- Practice sharing God's Word with others

OPENER (10 MINUTES)

[IMAGINATIVE, AUDITORY]

Have each of your students find a partner. The pairs will be working with Scripture references that deal with major truths by which many believers live. Give each pair a section of the **Words of Truth** repro page (page 76). They should come up with two truths and a lie about their given subject area. When your students are ready, have them get in a circle and play Two Truths and a Lie. See how many students choose the lies as truths. These may be some areas you could cover in future studies to strengthen their doctrine and faith. After a pair has revealed which one is the lie, have them share why it's a lie, based on the truth of God's Word.

Leaders need to take time to think through some of the lies they may hear that are not from God. It will help them become more discerning and teach them to keep their ears and hearts tuned in to God's truth. Nehemiah had to confront and expose lies during his ministry. A leader cannot remain resolved if he does not have a strong foundation of truth. There is no stronger foundation than God's Word. Psalm 119:105 states, "Your word is a lamp to my feet and a light for my path." God's Word is our standard and foundation for all we do.

IN THE WORD (10 MINUTES)

[ANALYTICAL, AUDITORY]

YOU'LL NEED

* Bibles

PEOPLE

Ezra is a fresh face in this book, but he has been busy on his own. Ezra has a passion for rebuilding the temple in Jerusalem, as well as an unbelievable respect for and ability to teach God's Word.

SETTING

This revival at the water gate is the first recorded revival meeting in Scripture.

TIME

The Feast of Tabernacles—otherwise known as the Feast of Booths—is a remembrance marking the beginning of the Jewish people's wanderings in the wilderness. It is also the beginning of the harvests (Leviticus 23:33-44).

BASIC OUTLINE

I. Practical Presentation (vv. 1-8)

    A. Reading and speaking

        1. Ezra reads to all who could understand.

        2. He reads from God's Word.

        3. He makes it clear to their understanding.

B. Respect and honor

    1. The words bring the people to their feet.

    2. The words bring them to worship.

    3. The words bring them to tears.

II. Powerful Information (vv. 9-12)

  A. Mourning

    1. Hearing God's Word convicts them of personal sins.

    (Note: The truth penetrates the heart, brings about a change from the inside out, and produces people of integrity.)

    2. The leaders, however, insist on being joyful in God's presence.

    (Note: The truth may be hard to take, but it's always the first step toward a deeper relationship with God and a life full of joy.)

  B. Encouragement

    1. The truth can be calming.

    2. There is joy in understanding the Word.

III. Personal Application (vv. 13-18)

  A. Desiring God's Word

    1. The people gather to hear and understand, especially the leaders.

    2. They make immediate application of the truth.

  B. Obedient to God's Word

    1. They do what is right regardless of what others have done.

    (Note: The people were resolved to do what was right because the truth was their foundation for living. The people had not been following the Jewish remembrances set up by Moses. They realized they should be doing the Feast of Tabernacles, and they got right on it.)

    2. They continue learning daily and obeying the truth that they hear.

TAKING ANOTHER LOOK (10 MINUTES)

[COMMON SENSE, AUDITORY]

Have your students divide themselves into small groups. Hand each group a copy of the **The Main Thing** repro page (page 77), something to write with, and a Bible. When

YOU'LL NEED

- Copies of the **The Main Thing** repro page (page 77), one for each small group
- Pencils or pens
- Bibles

most have finished answering the questions, have each group share a couple of their answers with everyone.

PRACTICAL EXPERIENCE (20 MINUTES)

OPTION 1: SHARING THE TRUTH [DYNAMIC, VISUAL]

YOU'LL NEED

• Bibles, one for each pair of students

• Sheets of paper, one for each pair of students

• Pencils or pens, for each pair of students

• Students' **Words of Truth** repro page (page 76)

Ask students to pair up and find passages of Scripture that contain a truth that's especially important to them. Then they should prepare to give a three-minute presentation to the rest of the group that includes a biblical truth, Scripture to back it up, and a practical application. You can suggest that they refer to their **Words of Truth** repro page (page 76) if they need inspiration for their presentations. Also, remind them of the points covered in Nehemiah 8 (i.e., practical presentation, powerful information, and personal application). Give students opportunities to share their truths during the session.

For further sharing opportunities, consider having your students prepare an object lesson to present along with their Scripture presentation, and possibly a song or another creative piece like a skit or puppet show they could share in a children's Sunday school class or during children's church. You could always brainstorm about other possibilities in order to give your student leaders the opportunity to practice teaching truth.

OPTION 2: WORD ART [DYNAMIC, KINESTHETIC]

YOU'LL NEED

• Copies of the **Words of Truth** repro page (page 76), one for each pair of students

• Pieces of cardboard or poster board, one for each pair of students

• Paint and paintbrushes

• Markers

• Old newspapers or bedsheets

Nehemiah had to be a man in line with God's Word and focused on God's will for his life. A leader cannot remain resolved if she does not have a strong foundation of truth. This activity has students thinking through some foundational truths from God's Word. It will help them to become more discerning and learn to keep their ears and hearts tuned to God's truth.

Have your students pair up and give each pair a section of the **Words of Truth** repro page (page 76). The pairs will be working with Scripture references that deal with major truths by which many believers live. After laying down some old newspapers or bedsheets to protect the floor, let each pair have a piece of cardboard and some paint. (You may also choose to use poster board and markers or any other artistic media you have available.) Each pair can get creative while making their own graffiti about God's truth. When your students are ready, have them all gather in a circle and discuss, in turn, why these Scripture truths are important, and how they might be able to relay these ideas to those around them.

Once their artwork has dried, plan to post them in visible locations around your youth room. This "word art" will be there to help students keep their focus on God's truth and his will for their lives as believers.

A FINAL WORD (10 MINUTES)

Have a short discussion with your students and ask the following questions:

* Do you have anyone in your life who will tell you the truth—no matter what?
* Share about a time when this person (or someone else) told you the truth, even when she knew it would be difficult for you to hear. How did you respond?
* What is your relationship like with that person today?
* How did the people respond when Ezra read the Word?
* Why is it important to have a daily focus on truth from God's Word?
* What can you do to ensure that truth is central to your life?
* What are some ways you can teach truth to those around you?

CLOSING PRAYER

Wrap up your time with a prayer like

God,

As believers, your Word has to be our foundation and center. Our relationship to you and the truth of your Word will influence how we deal with distractions, actively administrate, set the standard of integrity, and everything else we do. People need a standard, and there should be no other standard than your Word. May you help us to be leaders immersed in the truth of your Word!

Amen.

WORDS OF TRUTH

GOD'S PRESENCE

Where can I go from your Spirit? Where can I flee from your presence? If I go up to the heavens, you are there; if I make my bed in the depths, you are there. If I rise on the wings of the dawn, if I settle on the far side of the sea, even there your hand will guide me, your right hand will hold me fast. If I say, "Surely the darkness will hide me and the light become night around me," even the darkness will not be dark to you; the night will shine like the day, for darkness is as light to you. (Psalm 139:7-12)

GOD'S POWER

For God, who said, "Let light shine out of darkness," made his light shine in our hearts to give us the light of the knowledge of the glory of God in the face of Christ. But we have this treasure in jars of clay to show that this all-surpassing power is from God and not from us. We are hard pressed on every side, but not crushed; perplexed, but not in despair; persecuted, but not abandoned; struck down, but not destroyed. (2 Corinthians 4:6-9)

GOD'S WORD

"Sanctify them by the truth; your word is truth." (John 17:17)

"Your word is a lamp to my feet and a light for my path." (Psalm 119:105)

"For the word of God is living and active. Sharper than any double-edged sword, it penetrates even to dividing soul and spirit, joints and marrow; it judges the thoughts and attitudes of the heart." (Hebrews 4:12)

GOD'S LOVE

Who shall separate us from the love of Christ? Shall trouble or hardship or persecution or famine or nakedness or danger or sword? As it is written: "For your sake we face death all day long; we are considered as sheep to be slaughtered." No, in all these things we are more than conquerors through him who loved us. For I am convinced that neither death nor life, neither angels nor demons, neither the present nor the future, nor any powers, neither height nor depth, nor anything else in all creation, will be able to separate us from the love of God that is in Christ Jesus our Lord. (Romans 8:35-39)

THE MAIN THING

Ezra brings the truth to the people in this chapter. Think through the power of the truth that he shared and how that can and should affect your life and the lives of those around you.

1. What was the central part of all that Ezra and Nehemiah did?

2. How did the people respond?

3. How do you typically respond to hearing God's Word?

4. What can you do to make God's Word even more central in your life?

5. How will your relationship to the truth affect those around you? Your friends? Your family?

6. How can you share and teach truth to those around you?

7. In what ways will you begin doing this on a regular basis?

A LEADER HUNGERS FOR HOLINESS

SESSION 9: NEHEMIAH 9

OVERVIEW

This session is designed to encourage students to pursue holy lives.

During this session students will

- Learn to identify their need for holiness
- Understand how to make sure they are right with God
- Commit to a holy life before God

OPENER (10 MINUTES)

OPTION 1: THE PAINS OF HUNGER [IMAGINATIVE, VISUAL]

As you prepare for this session, be on the lookout for videos or programs that show the struggle many go through when they have little to no food to eat. There are many programs and mission agencies that have promotional videos you could use not only to show the true meaning of hunger, but also to encourage students to consider another ministry opportunity, to adopt a child as a group, or to raise

YOU'LL NEED

- A video about hunger from a mission organization or educational program money for those in need. (After all, they should already have a handle on actively administrating events and programs!) They might even consider going on a fast for a period of time to increase the awareness of the needs of others. (World Vision's 30 Hour Famine, for example, is an excellent way to raise the awareness of your students, church, and community, as well as the necessary funds to fight global hunger—www.30hourfamine.org.) However, this fast could also be from television, cell phone use, computer time, or anything else teenagers consider vital to their existence. But let your students choose what they'll do without and for how long.

After showing the video, ask—

- **Based on what you've just seen, how would you describe the pains of hunger?**
- **Has there ever been a time when you have truly hungered to be closer to God and in right standing before him?**
- **What would it take to bring you to the point of true hunger for holiness?**

Now say something like

You may have never felt the real physical pains of hunger as so many people do around the world each day. We should take time to thank God for his provision, as well as pray for the needs of others. However, we should all know the pains of spiritual hunger for holiness. Even more than a need for food, we need God. A godly leader needs to be a "needy" person when it comes to the things of God. In fact, in this chapter you will see the leaders taking center stage in the areas of learning and confession. Either way, we should keep in mind what it says in 1 Peter 1:15-16: "But just as he who called you is holy, so be holy in all you do; for it is written: 'Be holy, because I am holy.'" Nehemiah was truly a man who hungered for holiness.

OPTION 2: NEEDY EXPRESSIONS [IMAGINATIVE, KINESTHETIC]

YOU'LL NEED

- Whiteboard, overhead projector and transparency, or chalkboard

- Something to write with

Give each student 15 seconds to act out something that could be considered a need. You might even turn this into a game of charades between competing teams. Whatever you choose to do, on some object that all your students can see (e.g., a whiteboard, overhead transparency, or chalkboard) create a list of the needs that students come up with and discuss them further.

Questions to ask:

- **What do you think are the most important or basic needs on the list we've created?**
- **Why are those things so important?**
- **How important is this list of needs when compared to the things of God?**

Now say something like

We all have many basic and important needs in our lives. There are many things we cannot physically do without. Yet, even more than a need for food, we need God.

A godly leader needs to be a "needy" person when it comes to the things of God. In fact, in this chapter you will see the leaders taking center stage in the areas of learning and confession. Either way, we should keep in mind what it says in 1 Peter 1:15-16: "But just as he who called you is holy, so be holy in all you do; for it is written: 'Be holy, because I am holy.'" Nehemiah was truly a man who hungered for holiness.

IN THE WORD (10 MINUTES)

[ANALYTICAL, AUDITORY]

TIME

YOU'LL NEED

* Bibles

The people were concluding the Feast of Tabernacles by having a time of separation from their sins and any illegitimate relationships (as with foreigners), as well as confession of their sins. After this, there usually came a time of renewing their covenants to God.

BASIC OUTLINE

I. Separation and Confession (vv. 1-3)

    A. The people separate themselves from unbelievers.

    B. The people compare themselves to the truth of God's Word and confess.

II. Adoration and Consecration (vv. 4-38)

    A. The leaders give praise to God.

    B. They give adoration to God.

    C. They give thanks for what he did for them.

    D. They confess their sins.

    E. They recognize the consequences and judgment that is due.

    F. They commit their lives back to obedience to God.

(Note: Take note of how they went about their time of praise and repentance. These people were serious about becoming holy vessels for God.)

TAKING ANOTHER LOOK (15 MINUTES)

OPTION 1: STRIVING FOR HOLINESS
[COMMON SENSE, AUDITORY]

YOU'LL NEED

• Copies of the **Striving for Holiness** repro page (page 84), one for each small group

• Pencils or pens

• Bibles

Have your students divide into small groups and hand each a copy of the **Striving for Holiness** repro page (page 84), something to write with, and a Bible. Give them some time to answer the questions. When most of the groups have finished, have each share a couple of their answers with the rest of the group.

OPTION 2: CHARTING IT OUT
[COMMON SENSE, KINESTHETIC]

YOU'LL NEED

• Copies of the **Charting It Out** repro page (page 85), one for each student

• Copies of the students' letters from the Nehemiah 5 study

• Markers or colored pens, at least two different colors for each student

This activity gives your students the opportunity to be accountable to themselves for commitments they've made during past sessions. Pass out a copy of the **Charting It Out** repro page (page 85) to each student. At the same time, pass out the students' letters or purpose statements from the session on Nehemiah 5. Give your students time to review their letters to see how they've grown. Then have them take a marker and chart their progress. Using a different color marker, they should also mark where they'd like to be in another month. Tell them to set reasonable goals and continue to work until they get to where they feel God wants them to be.

PRACTICAL EXPERIENCE (20 MINUTES)

[DYNAMIC, AUDITORY]

YOU'LL NEED

• Copies of the biblical outline from the "In the Word" section, one for each group

• Bibles

This activity gives students an opportunity to work through prayers of confession. Nehemiah 9 isn't necessarily a hard and fast rule of how we should pray, but it is a good pattern to follow. Leaders need to be sure of their relationships with God in order to live holy lives before the people they lead.

Have your students get into groups of five or more and sit in circles. You may want to give each of the groups copies of the biblical outline from this session so students can refer to it during this activity. Ask your students to take turns within their groups, praying aloud in the manner outlined in the chapter. They can be as honest as they feel comfortable, but it will be a good opportunity to think through a prayer of confession.

When they are finished, have them share their thoughts on how this type of prayer could be important in their individual lives and share some of the areas they consecrated to God.

A FINAL WORD (10 MINUTES)

Have a short discussion with your students and ask the following questions:

- How often do you make confession a part of your prayer time?
- During the Feast of Tabernacles the leaders did six important things—gave praise to God, gave adoration to God, gave thanks for what God did for them, confessed their sins, recognized the consequences and judgment that was due, and committed their lives back to obedience to God. Which one of these six is the most difficult one for you to do? Which is the easiest? Explain.
- How often do you think a person should do these six steps?
- Why is it necessary for a leader to hunger for holiness?
- How can you ensure that you will keep the commitments you make to God?

CLOSING PRAYER

Wrap up your time with a prayer like

God,

Godly leaders need to hunger for holiness. If we are serious about being holy, we will begin working on the areas we've targeted. And then if we've done well, we should evaluate our lives to see how we can take things to the next level. Help us to pray daily for your help. People need leaders who are holy and serious about serving Christ. May you use us to encourage others to hunger for holiness in their own lives.

Amen.

STRIVING FOR HOLINESS

The work may be done on the outside—the city wall is finished—but there is still much that needs doing on the inside (in the people's hearts). The people all took a close look at their lives and made things right before God. We should do the same.

1. As you look over the passage, what comes first before we can get things right with God?

2. How did the people know what they were to confess?

3. How could they tell God had been with them, even when they were in the wrong?

4. What can you do to have a clear understanding of your relationship with God, and what you might need to confess?

5. What are some things from which you might need to separate yourself in order to keep your life pure and holy?

CHARTING IT OUT

On the graph below, use a marker or pen to draw a line that charts where you are in terms of meeting the integrity goals you set for yourself in session five. Then use a different color marker or pen and draw a line showing where you would like to be in one month's time. During the next few weeks, you can use this graph to chart your progress between now and a month from now.

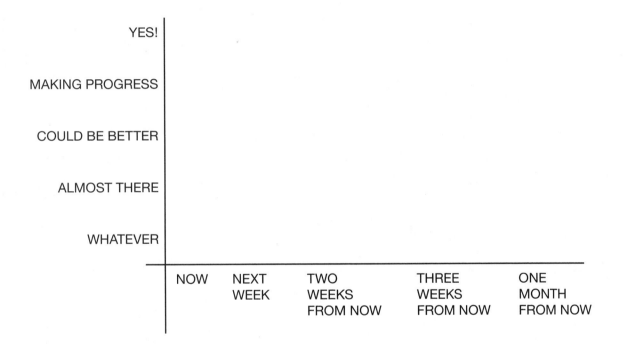

A LEADER WALKS THE WALK

SESSION 10: NEHEMIAH 10

OVERVIEW

This session is designed to challenge students to walk the Christian walk.

During this session students will

- Learn to identify their weak areas
- Understand the need for daily commitment
- Practice measuring their lives next to God's Word to find out when they're truly walking in faith—or just talking about it

OPENER (10 MINUTES)

OPTION 1: THINK BEFORE YOU WALK [IMAGINATIVE, AUDITORY]

Play "The Walk" by Steven Curtis Chapman.

While listening to the song, your students should pick up on what the people in the song were involved in, as well as the key to walking the walk.

YOU'LL NEED

- A copy of Steven Curtis Chapman's *Signs of Life* album (Sparrow/EMD, 1996)
- CD player

Questions to ask:

- **What positions do the four people in the song hold?**
- **What was key with the first two people?**
- **According to the Scripture used, how should we walk?**
- **Why do you think it all comes down to the walk?**

Now say something like

We can talk all day about what we should be doing as godly leaders. What really matters is how we live it out. Our walk has to match our talk if people are to follow us. Micah 6:8 states, "He has showed you, O man, what is good. And what does the Lord require of you? To act justly and to love mercy and to walk humbly with your God." A leader needs to truly live and walk out her faith.

OPTION 2: DOING THE WALK [IMAGINATIVE, KINESTHETIC]

YOU'LL NEED

• A handful of small rocks

Have a few willing students demonstrate their "cool walks" for the group. Discuss how each walk tells you something about that person. Next, have those same students walk again, except this time with small rocks stuck in their shoes. Have them do their best to do the cool walks again. Some may hide it well, but it will still hurt them.

Questions to ask:

- **What does a walk tell you about a person?**
- **How was it different walking with the rocks in your shoes?**
- **For those who were able to hide it, how did it affect you?**
- **If the rocks were never removed, would they eventually affect you? If so, how?**

Now say something like

We can be as cool as we want with our walk, but something as small as a pebble can hurt us—if not now, then definitely in the future. We need to be sure we're not trying to live lives for God while holding onto our sinful ways. They will come out eventually, and our walk has to match our talk if people are going to willingly follow us. Micah 6:8 states, "He has showed you, O man, what is good. And what does the Lord require of you? To act justly and to love mercy and to walk humbly with your God." A leader needs to truly live and walk out his or her faith.

IN THE WORD (10 MINUTES)

[ANALYTICAL, AUDITORY]

BACKGROUND

Several commitments the people made here in Jerusalem were all things they should have been doing from the very beginning:

* Intermarriage—the Jews were never to intermarry with the people of the surrounding and conquered nations (Deuteronomy 7:3).
* Business on the Sabbath—they were never to do any form of business on the Sabbath (Amos 8:5).
* Sabbatical Year—they were not to work the fields every seventh year (Exodus 23:10-11). They were also told to forgive all debts (Deuteronomy 15:1-2).
* Contribution to Temple Service—they committed to contribute one third of a shekel in this passage; however, they were originally told to give one half of a shekel (Exodus 30:13).
* Tithes—the people committed to offer the first of all their wealth and possessions to God for the care of the Levites, and the Levites were to give a tenth of those offerings directly to the priests for God's work (Numbers 18:21-26).

BASIC OUTLINE

I. The People (vv. 1-27)

  A. The leaders are represented by name.

  B. Nehemiah signs the covenant first.

  C. The people agree to the covenant with the leaders.

  (Note: The people agreed to follow their leaders and do no more than they were already supposed to be doing. Even so, it's best to at least get started!)

II. The Covenant (vv. 28-39)

  A. They commit to cease doing wrong.

      1. They join together to observe God's law.

  (Note: This was a public and national commitment.)

      2. They would not intermarry.

      3. They would not do business on the Sabbath day or other holy days.

      4. They would not work the fields every seventh year.

      5. They would cancel debts every seventh year.

B. They commit to learn how to do right.

    1. They would contribute financially to public worship.

    2. They would pay for materials used in worship.

    (Note: This would be costly, as they committed to purchase and offer the first and best of all their things for worship to God.)

    3. They would pay for compensation of worship leaders.

    (Note: Once again, they contributed the first portion of their personal income as a tithe to care for the leader; then they took care of their own personal expenses.)

    4. They would maintain the quality of worship and place of worship.

TAKING ANOTHER LOOK (10 MINUTES)

OPTION 1: LIVING THE WORD [COMMON SENSE, AUDITORY]

Have your students divide into small groups and hand each a copy of the **Living the Word** repro page (page 92), something to write with, and a Bible. When most of the groups have finished, ask each one to share a couple of its answers with everyone.

OPTION 2: COMPARED TO THE WORD [LEVEL-2] [COMMON SENSE, VISUAL]

This activity gives students the opportunity to express their thoughts about where they are in their walks and to identify areas they still need to work on. Pass out a copy of the **Compared to the Word** repro page (page 93) to each student. Next to each passage of Scripture, ask your students to draw symbols for how they feel they are doing in that area. Any symbol is fine as long as they know what it means. When they are done, tell them to take a moment to pray about those areas and ask for God's help in walking the walk.

PRACTICAL EXPERIENCE (20 MINUTES)

[DYNAMIC, KINESTHETIC]

This activity will provide your students with an ongoing assignment that will take their learning outside the youth room. It will be a great way to have direct accountability and practice living life by the Word.

YOU'LL NEED
- Copies of the **Living the Word** repro page (page 92), one for each small group
- Pencils or pens
- Bibles

YOU'LL NEED
- Copies of the **Compared to the Word** repro page (page 93), one for each student
- Pencils or pens

YOU'LL NEED
- Copies of the **Compared to the Word** repro page (page 93), one for each student
- Pencils or pens

Make sure each student has a copy of the **Compared to the Word** repro page (page 93), if each doesn't have one already. Students can choose to work in pairs. Have them brainstorm about how they can live out each passage of Scripture in everyday life. Then ask them each to choose adults they respect, ask those adults to observe them and write on students sheets how the students lived out the Word, and sign their names under the appropriate Scripture passages. When they are finished discussing, have a few students share their thoughts and plans to live out some of these verses.

Ask your students to bring their sheets to youth group in two weeks so they can review them with the group. (To make sure you actually have repro pages to review with your students during session 12, you may want to photocopy their completed pages before letting them take the pages home.)

A FINAL WORD (10 MINUTES)

Have a short discussion with your students and ask the following questions:

* **What is a *covenant?***
* **Name one or two leaders or teachers or other adults that you trust completely.**
* **If these people asked you to sign a covenant agreeing to follow a bunch of new rules, would you sign it? Explain your answer.**
* **Why is it important to walk the walk?**
* **What were the two basic steps the people of Jerusalem took to get things right?**
* **What should you do daily to be sure you're in line with God's Word?**
* **How do you plan to walk the walk from here on out?**

CLOSING PRAYER

Wrap up your time with a prayer like

God,

Leaders can't just be talkers—they need to be walkers of the Word. Nehemiah lived out a godly example for the people to follow, and he kept holiness a high priority in his life. We need to take time each day to examine our lives and be sure we are in line with your Word. Please help us as we work on weak areas and begin truly walking the walk.

Amen.

LIVING THE WORD

1. How do we know if we are walking the walk?

2. What were the two basic actions the people took to correct their walk?

3. What specifically did the people of Jerusalem cease to do?

4. What specifically did they commit to do?

5. How can you relate some of those areas to your personal life?

6. What was Nehemiah's example in this passage?

7. How will your walk affect those around you?

COMPARED TO THE WORD

GOD'S WORD

"Blessed is the man who does not walk in the counsel of the wicked or stand in the way of sinners or sit in the seat of mockers." (Psalm 1:1)

YOUR WALK

GOD'S WORD

"But his delight is in the law of the Lord, and on his law he meditates day and night." (Psalm 1:2)

YOUR WALK

GOD'S WORD

"He is like a tree planted by streams of water, which yields its fruit in season and whose leaf does not wither. Whatever he does prospers." (Psalm 1:3)

YOUR WALK

GOD'S WORD

"Each man should give what he has decided in his heart to give, not reluctantly or under compulsion, for God loves a cheerful giver." (2 Corinthians 9:7)

YOUR WALK

GOD'S WORD

"We have different gifts, according to the grace given us. If a man's gift is prophesying, let him use it in proportion to his faith. If it is serving, let him serve; if it is teaching, let him teach; if it is encouraging, let him encourage; if it is contributing to the needs of others, let him give generously; if it is leadership, let him govern diligently; if it is showing mercy, let him do it cheerfully." (Romans 12:6-8)

YOUR WALK

GOD'S WORD

"Therefore go and make disciples of all nations, baptizing them in the name of the Father and of the Son and of the Holy Spirit, and teaching them to obey everything I have commanded you. And surely I am with you always, to the very end of the age." (Matthew 28:19-20)

YOUR WALK

A LEADER PASSES ON THE POWER

OVERVIEW

The purpose of this session is to help students see the importance of training other leaders.

During this session students will

- Learn to identify the need for ownership
- Understand how to pass on the power to the next leader or leadership group
- Determine how and whom they will mentor

OPENER (10 MINUTES)

[IMAGINATIVE, KINESTHETIC]

Have students stand up to play a game of Simon Says. Play the game for a few minutes and then stop saying, "Simon says." After a few seconds, ask your students why they aren't doing anything. They will most likely say it's because you're not saying, "Simon says," or they'll ask if the game is over. Tell them the game isn't over, but you can't be Simon anymore. Have them discuss their options for continuing the game.

Questions to ask:

- **How will you keep playing the game?**
- **What can you do if there is no Simon?**
- **What should I have done to ensure the game would continue after I stopped playing?**

Now say something like

People need leadership, but they also need a sense of ownership to be able to take over the leadership when the original leader is gone. (By the way, you can tell them the game is over now.) **Those you lead also need to know how to lead themselves. Nehemiah had obviously brought the people to that point, as they began leading and administrating themselves. He did as we should, according to 2 Timothy 2:2, "And the things you have heard me say in the presence of many witnesses entrust to reliable men who will also be qualified to teach others." A leader knows how and when to pass the power on to the next person.**

IN THE WORD (10 MINUTES)

[ANALYTICAL, AUDITORY]

BASIC OUTLINE

YOU'LL NEED

* Bibles

I. Inhabiting the Land (vv. 1-19)

   A. They decide who will stay in Jerusalem and who will remain outside the city.

   B. They divide property among the individuals who will remain.

   C. People with varying talents, gifts, and abilities are staying.

   (Note: They especially focused on appointing leaders for protection of the city, as well as the spiritual health of the people who are remaining.)

II. Individual Leadership (vv. 20-36)

   A. Each family has its own area to lead.

   (Note: A leader initiates inclusiveness.)

   B. Each person leads according to his abilities.

      1. Some lead in the musical areas.

      2. Some serve as representatives for their communities.

   C. Each person leads his own home, whether inside or outside the walls.

   (Note: Integrity is the key to the individual family's leadership.)

TAKING ANOTHER LOOK (10 MINUTES)

OPTION 1: MAKING THE MOVE [COMMON SENSE, AUDITORY]

Have your students get into small groups. Give each group a copy of the **Making the Move** repro page (page 99), something to write with, and a Bible. When most of the groups have finished, ask each one to share a couple of its answers with everyone.

YOU'LL NEED

• Copies of the **Making the Move** repro page (page 99), one for each small group

• Pencils or pens

• Bibles

OPTION 2: AN INDEX OF LEADERSHIP [COMMON SENSE, VISUAL]

This activity gives students the opportunity to think through how they could train someone else to take over a leadership position. Give your students 10 index cards each. On one side of each card, ask them to write down one of the 10 leadership qualities they have learned about so far. They can work in pairs, but they will each need a set of cards. Then have your students put the cards in the order they would teach these qualities to someone else. (It doesn't have to be in the same order that you taught them.) Once they get their cards prioritized, discuss what they have done.

YOU'LL NEED

• 10 index cards for each student

• Pencils or pens

Questions to ask:

- **What do you feel are the most important qualities to teach?**
- **Why did you put the qualities in the order you did?**
- **How could teaching these qualities help train another leader?**

PRACTICAL EXPERIENCE (20 MINUTES)

[DYNAMIC, KINESTHETIC]

This activity gives students the opportunity to develop a plan to mentor a specific person to follow in their footsteps. It will certainly be a practical way to pass on the power. And don't forget what we learned in session 2!

YOU'LL NEED

• Students' half-completed index cards from the above activity or 10 blank index cards for each student

• Pencils or pens

Students will need the index cards they just used in the last activity. (If you chose Option 1, then you can now give 10 index cards to each student, along with some brief instructions as to what they should write on one side of each of their cards.) Be sure your students have the first 10 leadership qualities written on one side of their cards and that the cards are stacked in the order they would choose to teach someone else about these qualities. Now ask them to write on the blank side of each card specific ways they could train others to develop each leadership quality.

(Note: This next part is designed for your students who already serve in positions of leadership in your group or church. If you don't have any students who are currently leading others, you may wish to skip this last part for now.) When they are finished writ-

ing, have your students pray in pairs about whom they can begin mentoring over the next few weeks. Let them know that sometime during the next two weeks they will need to submit to you the names of people they intend to mentor.

A FINAL WORD (10 MINUTES)

Have a short discussion with your students and ask the following questions:

* **What personal qualities would you look for when choosing someone to mentor?**
* **Of the 10 leadership qualities we've discussed so far, which one do you think is the most important? Least important?**
* **As you think about mentoring someone to take over a leadership role, what do you imagine would be positive about that experience? What would be negative?**
* **Why is it important for a leader to give ownership and power to the people she leads?**
* **How were the people involved in leadership in Nehemiah 11?**
* **What can you do to be a leader who passes on the power?**
* **How can you plan to make that happen in the future?**

CLOSING PRAYER

Wrap up your time with a prayer like

God,

Strong leaders know how to choose and train other strong leaders to take their places. Nehemiah made sure every function of the city had leadership to keep things moving. Please continue to work in each of our hearts and minds as we pray about the people we may be mentoring in the days ahead.

Amen.

MAKING THE MOVE

1. Why wasn't Nehemiah mentioned in this passage? Why is it important that he wasn't?

2. How were other leaders involved?

3. What would be the need for new leadership?

4. How could you prepare those you lead to take over once you are gone?

5. What could you do right now to begin passing on the power to someone else?

OVERVIEW

The focus of this session is to recognize God for all he has done.

During this session students will

- Identify God's blessings
- Understand how to prepare for worship
- Praise God together

OPENER (10 MINUTES)

[IMAGINATIVE, VISUAL]

Have your students take out their **Compared to the Word** repro page (page 93) from Session 10 (or distribute the copies you made of their sheets during the last session). Discuss their progress in those areas and how they've accomplished their goals so far. Take time to praise God for their progress.

YOU'LL NEED

- Copies of students' **Compared to the Word** repro page (page 93) from Session 10

Questions to ask:

- **What are some areas of positive progress you have made in the last two weeks?**
- **How did you do it?**
- **Why is it important to recognize the forward progress in your life?**

Now say something like

God's blessings abound in our lives, but we seldom take time to give thanks and glorify him for those blessings. Nehemiah did a lot to prepare for a huge event that would glorify God. Hebrews 13:15 says, "Through Jesus, therefore, let us continually offer to God a sacrifice of praise—the fruit of lips that confess his name." A leader is always careful to thank and give glory to God.

IN THE WORD (10 MINUTES)

[ANALYTICAL, AUDITORY]

YOU'LL NEED

• Bibles

PEOPLE

Zerubbabel—according to Old Testament accounts, including the book of Ezra, he and Jeshua, the high priest, led a band of captives from Babylon to Jerusalem and began rebuilding the temple.

BASIC OUTLINE

I. Preparation of the People (vv. 1-26)

    A. A listing of several leaders who return to Jerusalem with Zerubbabel.

    B. The head Levites take their positions and are completely registered and legitimate.

    (Note: They continued to be concerned with purity and holiness.)

II. Dedication of the Wall (vv. 27-30)

    A. Everyone came together for the event.

    B. The priests and Levites purify themselves, the people, the gates, and the wall to prepare for worship.

III. Adoration of the Father (vv. 31-47)

    A. The people praise God with music.

(Note: There was a great amount of organization involved in preparing the leaders and people for singing. Also notice that verse 40 has a "so did I" in the middle of it. Nehemiah was in the midst of the people during the time of worship.)

B. The people praise God with offerings.

(Note: This included animal sacrifices, food, and money. And the people did so joyously and gratefully.)

C. The people praise God with their whole selves.

(Note: They performed a service before God and were compensated for their service. The Levites were also compensated and given charge over the money to care for the priests.)

TAKING ANOTHER LOOK (10 MINUTES)

OPTION 1: HEART OF WORSHIP [COMMON SENSE, AUDITORY]

Have your students divide into small groups and give each a copy of the **The Heart of Worship** repro page (page 106), something to write with, and a Bible. When most of the groups have finished working, have each share a couple of their answers with the rest of the group.

YOU'LL NEED

• Copies of the **Heart of Worship** repro page (page 106), one for each small group

• Pencils or pens

• Bibles

OPTION 2: GETTING YOUR FOCUS [COMMON SENSE, AUDITORY]

This activity gives students an opportunity to examine their lives and evaluate their motives for worshiping God. This will help prepare them for a time of genuine praise and worship. Play the song "Heart of Worship" by SonicFlood. Have your students reflect on how they have worshiped in the past, as well as how prepared they are for worship now.

Questions to ask:

* **What is involved in praise and worship time?**
* **Why is it necessary to prepare your heart?**
* **How do we ensure that all that we do still keeps God as our focus?**

YOU'LL NEED

• Copy of SonicFlood's self-titled album (Gotee Records, 1999)

• CD player

PRACTICAL EXPERIENCE (20 MINUTES)

OPTION 1: A PICTURE OF PRAISE [DYNAMIC, VISUAL]

YOU'LL NEED

• Poster board, one piece for each pair of students
• Old magazines
• Scissors
• Glue sticks
• Markers or pens

This activity gives students the opportunity to visually present their praises to God. Ask them to pair off and work together using poster board and a stack of old magazines to create a collage of praises to God. They can cut or tear out pictures that relate to their praise and write a caption under each one beginning with "I praise God for—".

When they have finished, have them share their praises with the rest of the group, and then take time to pray and give thanks. You might also consider hanging these collages in your youth room as a visible reminder of God's blessings and sovereignty.

OPTION 2: A SYMPHONY OF PRAISE [DYNAMIC, KINESTHETIC]

YOU'LL NEED

• Words and music for a variety of praise songs, hymns, or choruses

Let your students know you will be taking time to praise God for the things he has done. Just as in a musical symphony, there will be different segments—duets, solos, and group efforts—throughout the praise time. You might consider using your SonicFlood album as background during this time. Otherwise, you might take favorite praise songs, hymns, or choruses to sing together in between each time of praise. *(You could actually assign the leadership of this time to a musical leader in your group.)*

Use the following outline for your Symphony of Praise.

1. As a group, praise God out loud for who he is. You can do popcorn prayer with this segment. (2 minutes)
2. Individually and silently, ask God to forgive you for any areas that are still not right in your relationship with him. (2 minutes)
3. In pairs, praise God for his power to change us and mold us into the image of his Son. (2 minutes)
4. Get into groups of three or four to share praises with each other, and praise God through prayer for things he has done in your life. (5 minutes)
5. In pairs again, pray a prayer to dedicate your life to God and commit to glorifying him on a daily basis. (2 minutes)

You can close things up with a final prayer to dedicate the group.

A FINAL WORD (10 MINUTES)

Have a short discussion with your students and ask the following questions:

- **Name a few (personal) reasons to praise God today.**
- **Why is it so important to seriously praise and glorify God?**
- **How did the people glorify God in this passage?**
- **Which of these ways of praising God (with music, offerings, and whole selves) is the easiest for you to do? The most difficult? Explain your answers.**
- **What should you do as you prepare for worship?**
- **In what ways can you glorify and praise God on a daily basis?**
- **Share some examples of how you might praise God with your whole self.**

CLOSING PRAYER

Wrap up your time with a prayer like

God,

Nothing in Jerusalem could have been done apart from your power and sovereignty. Nehemiah was careful to recognize that, and he led the people in a very public worship of you. We need to be at the forefront of praising and worshiping you at every opportunity we get. Please help us with that in the days ahead.

Amen.

THE HEART OF WORSHIP

1. How did the people prepare for worship?

2. What are some things you should consider as you personally prepare for worship?

3. In what ways did the people praise God?

4. What are some specific ways you can praise God with your talents and gifts?

5. What are some reasons you have for praising God in such an involved way?

A LEADER CONTINUES CONTACT
BONUS SESSION: NEHEMIAH 13

OVERVIEW

This session is designed to encourage students to keep in touch with those they lead.

During this session students will

- Learn to identify when it's time for them to bow out
- Understand how to appropriately confront or provide advice
- Begin some form of consistent contact with those they may be currently leading

(Note: You may want to begin this session by collecting the names of the people your leaders will be mentoring. You will also want to schedule a time to review the progress of each mentoring relationship. Continuing contact is what this session is all about!)

OPENER (10 MINUTES)

[IMAGINATIVE, VISUAL]

YOU'LL NEED

* A large mixing bowl
* Cake ingredients (cake mix, eggs, oil)
* A measuring cup
* Spoon

Mix the cake ingredients together in a bowl and offer the cake batter to the group. This obviously won't be the best of cakes. Only half the work is done. A cook needs to follow through with baking, checking on the progress from time to time, and icing it before the cake is ready to be consumed. If a cake is taken out too soon or left unchecked, it could come out of the oven a sloppy mess or burned.

Discuss this process with the group. Ask—

- **What needs to be done with the cake in order to enjoy it?**
- **What if I don't check on it from time to time while it's baking?**
- **If a leader doesn't check in on new leadership, what could happen?**

Now say something like

We all need accountability and support. A leader needs to continue contact with those he leaves behind. Proverbs 13:20 says, "He who walks with the wise grows wise, but a companion of fools suffers harm." A leader will provide that wisdom and insight by keeping in touch with those who have taken over.

YOU'LL NEED

* Bibles

IN THE WORD (10 MINUTES)

[ANALYTICAL, AUDITORY]

BACKGROUND

When the people were reading the Scriptures at the beginning of this chapter, they had been reading from Deuteronomy 13:3-5:

> You must not listen to the words of that prophet or dreamer. The Lord your God is testing you to find out whether you love him with all your heart and with all your soul. It is the Lord your God you must follow, and him you must revere. Keep his commands and obey him; serve him and hold fast to him. That prophet or dreamer must be put to death, because he preached rebellion against the Lord your God, who brought you out of Egypt and redeemed you from the land of slavery; he has tried to turn you from the way the Lord your God commanded you to follow. You must purge the evil from among you.

The people were not to follow the advice of false prophets or leaders, but carefully to consider the commandments of God.

BASIC OUTLINE

I. Reexamine the Word (vv. 1-3)

    A. Examines the Word once again.

B. Excludes all foreigners from Israel to maintain purity.

(Note: The people used God's Word as the foundation for their decisions.)

II. Reexamine the Leadership (vv. 4-9)

A. Eliashib had not taken care of Levites, priests, and other leaders.

B. Nehemiah returns to set things straight.

(Note: Nehemiah directly confronts the sin.)

III. Reexamine the Administration (vv. 10-14)

A. Nehemiah restores order among the people.

(Note: He confronts their commitment to care for their spiritual leaders.)

B. The tithe is replenished.

C. Nehemiah chooses new leadership.

IV. Reexamine the Commitments (vv. 15-22)

A. Nehemiah stops the work on the Sabbath.

B. He reminds them of the disaster brought on their forefathers for this same wrongdoing.

(Note: He confronts them with their history.)

C. Nehemiah sets up guard and locks down the city on the Sabbath.

(Note: Drastic measures need to be taken to maintain purity.)

V. Reexamine the Purity (vv. 23-29)

A. Nehemiah reprimands those who had intermarried.

B. He reminds them of Solomon's troubles because of this same wrongdoing.

(Note: He confronts them with the failures of their heroes.)

C. Nehemiah even expels a priest for intermarrying.

VI. Reexamine the Praise (vv. 30-31)

A. Nehemiah completes the purification of the people.

B. He asks God to remember him for good.

(Note: Nehemiah always wanted the blessing of God. God was the number one priority.)

TAKING ANOTHER LOOK (20 MINUTES)

OPTION 1: KEEPING IN TOUCH [COMMON SENSE, AUDITORY]

Have students get into small groups and hand each one a copy of the **Keeping in Touch** repro page (page 112). Give each group time to answer the questions. When most of the groups have finished, have each group share a couple of their answers with everyone.

OPTION 2: CONFRONTING CONFRONTATION [COMMON SENSE, KINESTHETIC]

This activity provides practice in thinking through and appropriately confronting sinful practices in love. Ahead of time, write a variety of sinful patterns on slips of paper. Then fold and deposit them into a hat or bowl.

Have students divide into groups of two or three. Ask them to choose a scenario from the hat and come up with a role play to illustrate it to the rest of the group. Then your students can role-play the situations while following a rough outline from the passage.

You can use the following thoughts to share with your students how they can confront these sinful practices:

- God's Word as a foundation for their confrontation
- Directly confront the sinful pattern
- Remind them of their commitments
- Provide an example of consequences related to this type of practice in others' lives
- Present a plan of action for change
- Pray; always give it over to God

PRACTICAL EXPERIENCE (10 MINUTES)

[DYNAMIC, KINESTHETIC]

This activity gets your students ready to commit to working with and training others to lead for the cause of Christ. It also provides them with a great example of a way to keep in touch.

Have students think about the people they've agreed to mentor. Have them write letters to those people, outlining their commitments to keep in contact with them, as well as specific plans to keep in touch (e.g., when and where to meet, how often, and so on). When they are finished, have them share their ideas with the rest of the group. Then leave it up to them to pass the letters along to the other people.

YOU'LL NEED

- Copies of **Keeping in Touch** repro page (page 112), one for each small group
- Pencils or pens

YOU'LL NEED

- A hat or other container
- Slips of paper with a sinful pattern written on each one
- Bibles

YOU'LL NEED

- Sheets of paper, one for each student
- Pencils or pens
- Letters, one for each student, that you have prepared ahead of time

Meanwhile, you can use this time to pass out the personal letters you have written to each of your students, outlining your commitment to keep in touch and be available to them whenever they need you. Be sure to be specific and honest. A true leader leads by example!

A FINAL WORD (10 MINUTES)

Have a short discussion with your students and ask the following questions:

- **How can you use the Bible to help you in your leadership role?**
- **What did Nehemiah do after he left Jerusalem?**
- **How do you appropriately deal with sinful practices?**
- **Why is it necessary to keep in touch with those you lead?**
- **How can you plan to continue contact with those you've mentored?**
- **Is God the number one priority in your life and leadership? Explain your answer.**
- **If not, what can you do today to make God the number one priority in your life and leadership?**

CLOSING PRAYER

Wrap up your time with a prayer like

God,

Nehemiah has given us a wonderful, godly example of true leadership. Keeping in contact is so important, yet it is just one of the many building blocks to biblical leadership. We would do well to review this material again and read over the Book of Nehemiah on a regular basis to see how our leadership compares to that of biblical leadership according to your Word. Please help us to go out and be the leaders we need to be for the cause of Jesus Christ.

Amen.

KEEPING IN TOUCH

1. What can happen when a leader leaves after she's passed on the power?

2. Why do situations like that occur?

3. What can a leader do to help the situation?

4. How should a leader respond to a sinful practice?

5. What are the keys for a leader to keep in mind when confronting a problem?

APPENDIX

SCRIPTURE MEMORY LIST

WEEK 1

"The prayer of a righteous man is powerful and effective." (James 5:16)

WEEK 2

"Do not those who plot evil go astray? But those who plan what is good find love and faithfulness."(Proverbs 14:22)

WEEK 3

"Then make my joy complete by being like-minded, having the same love, being one in spirit and purpose." (Philippians 2:2)

WEEK 4

"Let us fix our eyes on Jesus, the author and perfecter of our faith, who for the joy set before him endured the cross, scorning its shame, and sat down at the right hand of the throne of God." (Hebrews 12:2)

WEEK 5

"Search me, O God, and know my heart; test me and know my anxious thoughts. See if there is any offensive way in me, and lead me in the way everlasting." (Psalm 139:23-24)

WEEK 6

"You, dear children, are from God and have overcome them, because the one who is in you is greater than the one who is in the world." (1 John 4:4)

WEEK 7

"But everything should be done in a fitting and orderly way."
(1 Corinthians 14:40)

WEEK 8

"Your word is a lamp to my feet and a light for my path." (Psalm 119:105)

WEEK 9

"But just as he who called you is holy, so be holy in all you do; for it is written: 'Be holy, because I am holy.'" (1 Peter 1:15-16)

WEEK 10

"He has showed you, O man, what is good. And what does the Lord require of you? To act justly and to love mercy and to walk humbly with your God." (Micah 6:8)

WEEK 11

"And the things you have heard me say in the presence of many witnesses entrust to reliable men who will also be qualified to teach others." (2 Timothy 2:2)

WEEK 12

"Through Jesus, therefore, let us continually offer to God a sacrifice of praise—the fruit of lips that confess his name." (Hebrews 13:15)

WEEK 13

"He who walks with the wise grows wise, but a companion of fools suffers harm." (Proverbs 13:20)

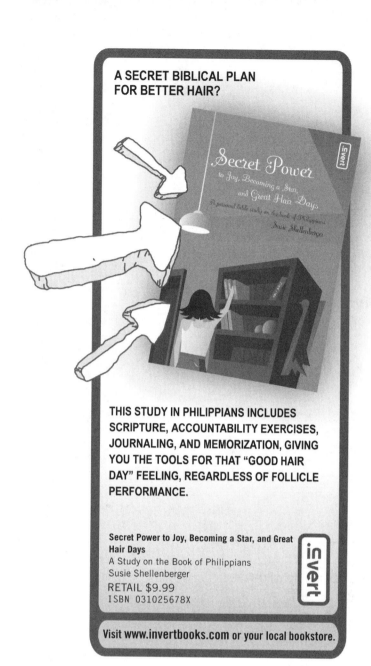